Harrison Design Associates
A DECADE OF WORK

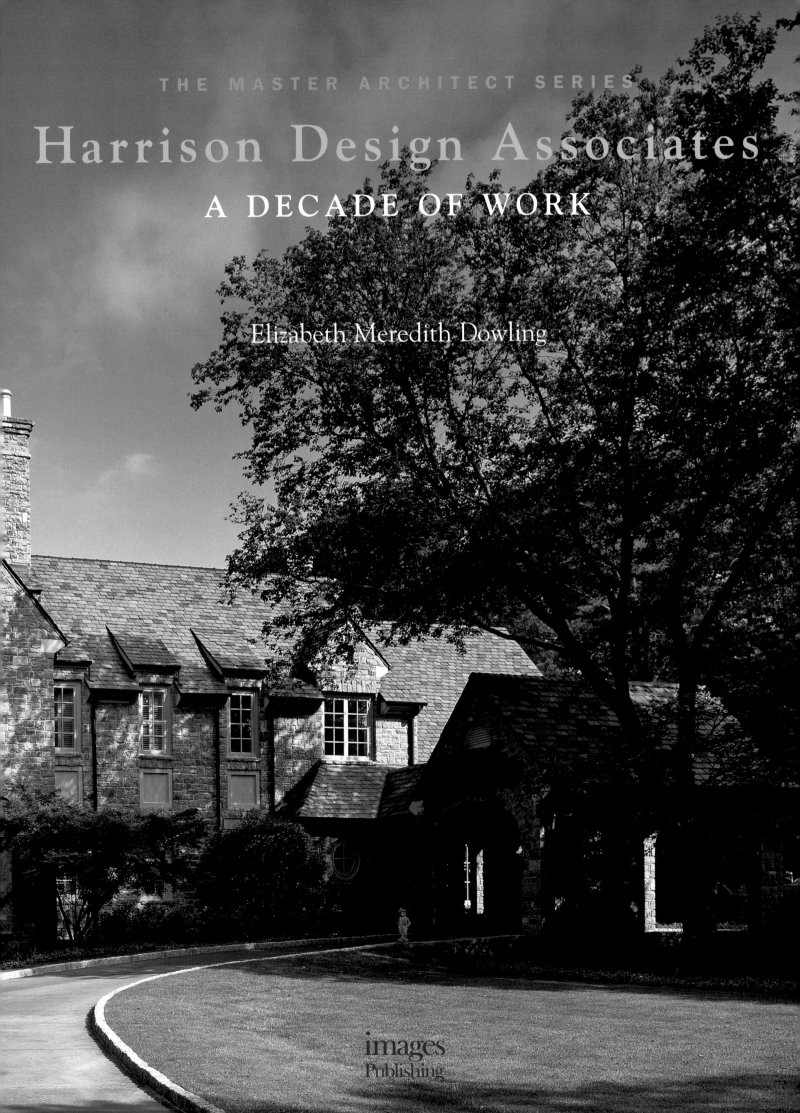

Harrison Design Associates

A DECADE OF WORK

Elizabeth Meredith Dowling

images
Publishing

Published in Australia in 2007 by
The Images Publishing Group Pty Ltd
ABN 89 059 734 431
6 Bastow Place, Mulgrave, Victoria 3170, Australia
Tel: +61 3 9561 5544 Fax: +61 3 9561 4860
books@imagespublishing.com
www.imagespublishing.com

National Library of Australia Cataloguing-in-Publication entry:

Dowling, Elizabeth Meredith.
Harrison Design Associates : a decade of work.

ISBN 9781864702774 (hbk.).

1. Harrison Design Associates. 2. Architecture, Domestic – United States.
3. Architectural firms – United States. I. Harrison Design Associates.
II. Title. (Series: Master architect series).

728.0973

Coordinating editor: Robyn Beaver

Designed by The Graphic Image Studio Pty Ltd, Mulgrave, Australia
www.tgis.com.au

Digital production by Splitting Image Colour Studio Pty Ltd, Australia
Printed by Everbest Printing Co Ltd in Hong Kong/China

IMAGES has included on its website a page for special notices in relation to this
and our other publications. Please visit www.imagespublishing.com

Contents

7 Foreword
by Paul Gunther, President,
The Institute of Classical Architecture & Classical America

9 Introduction
by Elizabeth Meredith Dowling

12 Paces End Manor

24 Cima Vista

36 Hawn Residence

50 Paces End Estate

60 Georgian Residence

70 Riddle Beach Retreat

80 English Manor

90 Hacienda Hermosa

102 Cohen Lake Retreat

112 All'Ombra

124 Spring Hill Farm

136 Echols Residence

146 Miller Residence

156 Acheson Residence

172 Sturm Residence

182 Cannon Residence

190 Azalea House Renovation

202 West Paces Village Overview

212 Richardson-Franklin House Renovation

220 Erbesfield Residence

231 Other notable projects

242 Projects in process

250 Acknowledgments

Foreword

In February 2007, I had the privilege to help recognize the inaugural winners of the Shutze Awards at an auspicious annual function of the Institute of Classical Architecture & Classical America's (ICA&CA) Southeast Chapter.

As a lively regional complement to the Arthur Ross Awards for Excellence in the Classical Tradition, the Shutze laureates together provided a glimpse of regional achievement for specific recent projects across related categories, describing as they did the health and well-being of the classical tradition today as one critical part of contemporary American practice. This Southeast Chapter initiative did not obviate Arthur Ross Award winners from the according geographic area; on the contrary, as the long record of winners reveals (Philip Trammell Shutze after all was the first architect recipient of a Ross Award at the event's 1982 advent), it helped bring to further nationwide attention those at the forefront of this dynamic quadrant.

I was further gladdened by the fact that the Shutze awardee in the category of *Multi-family Residence* was received by the Atlanta-based firm of Harrison Design Associates, the group of exemplary practitioners whose residential work is the deserving subject of this book.

It was in particular the firm's Inman Park Village Row Houses that were selected by the jury as outstanding. And yet what was evident to one and all was how these historically resonant urban homes exemplified a broad body of work that has for so long set a standard of design and civic merit. The design solution for Inman Park Village does not imitate the past; instead through careful research of classical precedent and its local vernacular interpretation, it is a modern solution intended for the sake not only of those destined to inhabit the structure, but also the surrounding community and the streets defining it—well served as they are by the relation of structure, nature, and human scale. The Row Houses are thus a metaphor—a gateway for examination and appreciation. The contents of this volume will, I believe, prove my point best of all and I join in welcoming the revelation of its contents.

What is perhaps less evident is the leadership of Harrison Design Associates on behalf of contemporary classicism generally. In addition to a trail-blazing role in the creation of the Southeast Chapter in 2004—as what proved to be a national prototype—Bill, as a generous and peripatetic board member, helped to forge and implement an agenda of exemplary academic and programmatic innovation sustaining the classical tradition in architecture, town planning, and their allied fine and applied arts, as well as building crafts, both for the present day and for many challenging years to come.

The essential rules of classicism in practice, theory, and manual skills and their manifestation in the built environment have brought promise almost unthinkable a generation ago. These rules need to be known whether to break them anew or, as in the case of the Institute, to interpret and apply them for a sustainable and humane American future.

This effort is best revealed with the 2007 arrival of a Master of Science in Architecture Degree with Concentration in Classical Design offered by Georgia Tech in dynamic partnership with the ICA&CA. Harrison Design Associates led the way in tandem with Professor Elizabeth Dowling of the Institute's Council of Advisors and her Georgia Tech College of Architecture faculty colleagues. It is a model of pedagogy bringing to bear the Institute's well-established core curriculum within the overall academic offering of a leading American university. Like the Southeast Chapter, its visionary example heralds widespread promise for contemporary practice. It too sets a standard, in this instance, for innovative education in the 21st century.

The design achievement to be discovered in these pages is in my view further enhanced when taken in the context of this larger educational and civic contribution. Readers of this volume are well advised to take stock of this historic development and measure it against the momentum it unleashes.

Plato wrote in *The Republic,* "The direction in which education starts a man will determine his future life." By teaching the underlying principles of classicism in new ways—and to an eager new student community—the Institute and those like Harrison Design Associates who guide its future course, sustain the possibility of such a rich career pathway. Doors of past discovery are opened and made current in a continuum of knowledge too precious to discard as those who draw actively from the classical tradition now understand.

Paul Gunther
President
The Institute of Classical Architecture & Classical America

Introduction

As leaders in the field of residential design, partners William (Bill) Harrison, Gregory (Greg) Palmer, and Anthony (Tony) Spann produce not only fine architecture, but they also devote enormous energy to ensuring the continued growth of classical and traditional design in the United States. Success in this goal is measured on the local and national levels through support of students and classes at the Georgia Institute of Technology, the national and southeast chapter of The Institute of Classical Architecture & Classical America (ICA&CA), and consistent sponsorship of charitable events. Their Atlanta firm has expanded in recent years to include offices in St. Simons Island, Georgia, and California offices in Santa Barbara and Beverly Hills.

The path to the founding and continued life of this vibrant architectural practice was not the typical route taken by architects. Their combined backgrounds enriched the knowledge of the three partners, thus enabling them to apply years of practical knowledge to the prolific work that makes theirs one of the largest classical and traditional firms in the nation.

As a young teen, Bill worked as a draftsman. Following this experience, he concluded that he would study architecture and he selected the highly respected program at the Georgia Institute of Technology. The head of the school in the 1960s, Paul M. Heffernan FAIA, had won the 28th Paris Prize and studied at the Ecole des Beaux-Arts from 1935 to 1938, but the German Bauhaus equally influenced him. Heffernan's numerous buildings on the Georgia Tech campus, including the architecture building, demonstrated an easy alliance between Beaux-Arts planning and superficial Bauhaus detailing. In his required theory class, Heffernan shared his respect for history past and present with his design students. Influenced by Heffernan's eclectic interests after leaving Georgia Tech, Bill embarked on a journey to experience world architecture. Unlike some fields of academic inquiry, architecture is a three-dimensional art that reflects the character of its context. Materials, detailing, and climate have historically shaped the choices architects made in the creation of buildings. These aspects cannot be understood solely through study and reading—they must be experienced first-hand.

Ultimately, his study tour turned into a five-year journey of self-discovery. He experienced urban and country buildings throughout most of Europe and North and South America.

He worked with various architects during his travels and recorded details that he would later use in the work of his firm. Especially evident in his work are the details he recorded in Italy, Spain, France, and England. The work of Andrea Palladio deeply impressed him, so he systematically visited all of his villas and palazzos in Vicenza and the surrounding Veneto. Later in his journey, he compared the original work to the 18th-century Palladian-inspired houses in England and determined that he preferred the original sources to the northern interpretation. During his visit to the Villa Barbaro in Maser, he was profoundly impressed by the self-confidence Palladio expressed in his use of materials and his inclusion of humorous details in an otherwise serious study of ideal beauty. Bill credits the revelations of this day as the moment he decided to become an architect.

Greg Palmer has a keen understanding of the making of architecture. His knowledge developed from his youth spent following, and later working for, his father and grandfather—both general contractors. He pursued his architectural training at the Southern Technical Institute located near Atlanta. Although this program's philosophy was based in modernism, the faculty allowed students the freedom to explore the use of traditional styles in their designs. His design approach was shaped by his extensive practical knowledge gained from his family's contracting business combined with his interest in historic architecture. This varied background created an ability to produce well-crafted buildings made with authentic period details that incorporate both local and exotic materials. Greg's combined interest in construction and architecture caused him to become both a licensed architect and building contractor—a most unusual combination. Greg continues the process of lifelong learning with focused study and drawing tours of favorite European architects such as Sir Edwin Lutyens. From the study of these excellent examples of history, and his direction of the consistently expanding resource library of rare books and recent architectural publications, he brings new character to the firm's work.

Tony Spann grew up in the architectural environment of Chicago and more specifically the community of Riverside—the suburban development internationally known for the work of Frederick Law Olmsted and Frank Lloyd Wright. His father, like Greg's, had a family construction business.

He, too, accompanied his father on visits to construction sites and, beginning with youthful jobs, started as a laborer and carpenter, and then advanced to project superintendent, construction manager, and project estimator. Influenced by the architectural heritage of Chicago, he decided to become an architect and studied at the University of Illinois, one of the premier design schools in the country during those years. After graduation, he relocated to California and established his own design firm in Santa Barbara in 1986.

Bill Harrison founded his design firm in 1991, and his partner, Greg Palmer joined the firm in 1995. With the opening of the Santa Barbara office, Tony Spann joined the firm as a principal and managing partner of the California office in 2004. Each of the partners brings an individual strength to the firm that creates an exceptional unity. The partners share a vision of architecture that is both modern and traditional. The aesthetic preferences of the architects are not limited to a particular period or style, but encompass all that fall within the realm of humanist architecture. They also share a belief that architects of all periods have employed the latest technology in their buildings and excellence in fundamental construction and detailing characterizes their work. From their earliest work experience, all three have developed extensive knowledge of construction as well as design.

To achieve the many scales of projects from single-family in-town bungalows to palatial estates, from large-scale urban planning to infill townhouses, and from new to restored civic and ecclesiastical designs, the large four-office firm is organized as individualized *ateliers* or studios. The atelier is a French concept of educational organization derived from the Ecole des Beaux-Arts, the renowned architectural school. Originally, the *atelier* referred to a group of students who banded together to learn architecture by inviting a successful architect to visit their studio space and criticize their design efforts. In current American terminology, both atelier and studio refer to a group of designers who work as a team to draw upon each other's strengths and produce optimal design solutions. In this organizational model, the large firm becomes a series of small groups that can devote individual attention to every client. The result is a more personal response to each of a large number of simultaneously developing buildings. This

system also allows them to take advantage of shared office resources and ideas of the group from the most experienced architect to the budding intern.

The partners agree that in addition to efficiency, other positive results of the atelier system include the ability to address the many stylistic choices of their clients. According to Tony Spann, "This system has had the positive effect of our firm producing a variety of architectural styles." The work in the California office reflects the character of the West Coast and typically includes references to the ornate Spanish Baroque, or the simplified forms of the Spanish Mission influence, or the early 20th-century modernist movement. Greg Palmer says, "There's a place at the table for all forms of architecture as long as there is sensitivity to the environment and honesty in materials." Bill Harrison believes, "Good architecture is not about a style, it is about substance. Classical design is a living, breathing, and evolving form that uses the past as a foundation to create a vocabulary that reflects our moment in time." Greg continues, "Good design does not slavishly copy past forms—it must have a sense of place and time. Past works are used to inform today's architecture."

Education remains a hallmark of the firm's philosophy and philanthropic work. The firm regularly hires interns and assists them in furthering their own understanding of architecture. Internship is a recognized period of training for the future architect. Prior to taking extensive registration examinations, an aspiring architect must receive an accredited professional college degree and then work with an architect for a period of years as specified by different states. Within this firm, a mentor who is one of the project architects carefully guides the professional growth of each young employee through the period of internship. This more experienced individual assigns tasks that ensure opportunities for all members of the team to learn to communicate with clients, other professionals in the construction process and office colleagues. The respectful philosophy of the firm guides all members to approach their work as "we" and not "I." Greg says, "We all feel the same way—when our careers are complete, we want to be judged in equal measure by the quality of the work we produced and by our contribution to the lives of employees, clients, and allied professionals."

The firm also extends these efforts to the community. The partners believe it is important to help educate a public that has lost connection to the built world and does not value architecture due, in large measure, to current design philosophy. The partners state:

Over the years, often in a desire to create something 'new' or 'revolutionary,' designers have cast aside proven classical design principles. Sadly, the result is a compromised built environment filled with examples of bad design in residential, commercial, and even institutional works that were once the cherished bastions of design integrity. A public that at one time would have rejected this work has unfortunately become desensitized to careless architecture and slowly they are losing the ability to recognize basic elements of good and bad design. The question we pose to ourselves is, "How do we turn the tide of architectural apathy and ignorance?"

In addressing this question, one response formulated by the firm is the support for college education at the Georgia Institute of Technology. In 2002, the partners initiated the *Harrison Design Associates Visiting Scholar in Classical Design* program. The presence of these visiting scholars added diversity of opinion and of design philosophy to the nationally recognized College of Architecture that is best known in professional circles for its modernist architecture. Through the Visiting Scholars program, architecture students are given access to design studios and elective classes that address a wide array of issues not currently provided in the curriculum. The first visitor was local Atlanta architect Eugene Surber who is nationally recognized for his work in historic preservation. In subsequent years the scholars have included Anne Fairfax and Richard Sammons, partners in the New York and Palm Beach firm of Fairfax and Sammons; Gregory Saldana, president of Saldana Design & Preservation Inc. from Boston and Miami; and Christine Franck, whose office is in New York. These visiting scholars have conducted classes in the design of houses, infill construction in Charleston, South Carolina, and a study of classical systems of proportion. The firm's ongoing support has most recently assisted in the creation of the country's first Master of Science degree in Classical Design. This one-year degree allows students to study in both New York City and Atlanta. This new degree is seen as a creative opportunity to heal the rift between classical and modernist architecture that has existed for more than half a century.

The philosophy of the firm has shaped the projects that follow. These selected buildings represent the many design styles and project types with which the firm is involved. Although there is great diversity in the stylistic appearance of the work, the consistency of its buildings lies in the demand for finely detailed projects, excellent materials, and lasting construction. The most highly skilled craftsmen in stone and wood assist in the creation of the buildings. A deep knowledge of materials will be seen in the use of both local and imported materials that are selected for their color range, texture, or association with place. The diversity of its work reflects the firm's belief that architects should focus on fulfilling the architectural desires of their clients. This attitude differs from many modernist designers' sense of aesthetic superiority that encourages them to place their personal desires above the interests of the public at large. Bill says, "It is our goal for our homes to be a reflection of our clients' preferences and style. Our task is to take our clients' dreams and through collaboration make them better than they could have possibly imagined."

Elizabeth Meredith Dowling

Paces End Manor
Atlanta, Georgia, 2001

Located on extensive lands appropriate to the design inspiration of an English Manor House, this site is carefully zoned for private and public access. The house is entered from a circling arrival court from which the family can also gain access, through a covered passageway, to the parking court and garages. The main body of the house has an irregular outline of gabled masses and what appear to be later intersecting building additions. This set of elements gives the impression that the building has undergone a series of changes over a lengthy history, while in fact the house was built all at once. The aged appearance of the house is achieved through its materials of tumbled weathered brick laid with flush mortar joints and pitted cast stone over which English ivy has been trained to grow in specific locations. These combinations create the roughened appearance that would otherwise take centuries of weathering to produce.

The main entry, marked with a segmental arch in cast stone, gives access to the open foyer and living room axis that terminates in views of the private gardens beyond. A cross-hall opens to the stair and dining room through freestanding twin and attached Doric columns. The broad segmental arched openings and semicircular arches on columns balance a sense of defined space with the flowing quality of a free plan. The main stair rises past a stepped leaded-glass window with stone mullions through which dappled light is cast into the dining area.

The English Manor theme determines the interior detailing of vaulted and timbered ceilings, iron lighting fixtures and heavy timber doors. The family room ceiling is supported on the medieval detailing of pegged wood hammerbeam trusses; a high corbeled balcony gives views to the space below. Access to the game room is by a massive door ornamented with iron and brass fittings. A shallow brick vaulted passage leads to the antique timbered ceiling of the game room with its iron-strapped pine bar resembling one found in English pubs.

Previous pages
   A picturesque vision of irregular massing surrounds the arrival court
Opposite
   The lengthy curving drive ends with an encompassing view of the house complex
1   Site plan

1

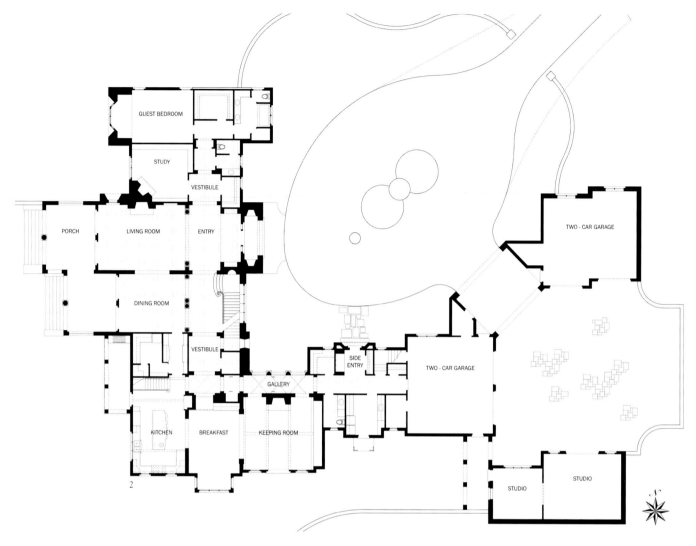

2

2   Main floor plan
3   An arcade on twin columns separates the dining room from the cross-hall and principal stair
4   The dining room spatially flows into the living room through the segmental arched opening

3

4

5   The main entry is marked with a two-story composition uniting the covered
    porch and triple windows above
6   The main entry indicating complex stone detailing
7   A variety of arched openings ornament all four sides of the living room;
    here, the arched mahogany doors lead to a covered porch

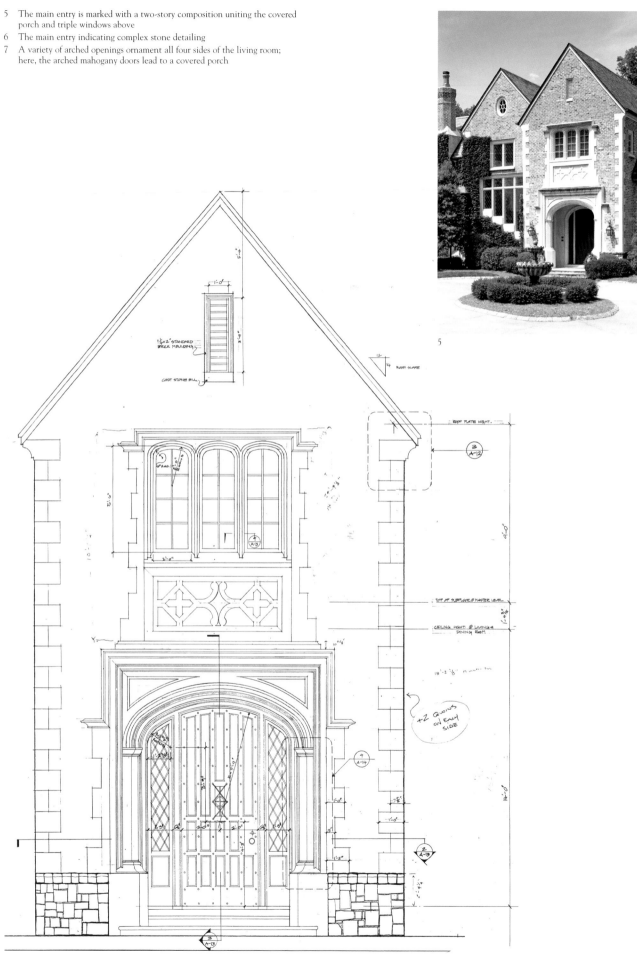

5

6

8   A heavy timber door with iron and brass fittings opens to the game room
Opposite
    Heavy timbers with pegged joints support the ceilings of the family room and
    breakfast room beyond

8

10   Covered porch adjacent to the living room
11   Field House
12   Corner view toward the bay window of the breakfast room and the covered entry to the kitchen

10

11

12

Cima Vista
Montecito, California, 2004

The inspiration for this house derived from the general architectural themes of historic Santa Barbara Spanish Revival and the California Arts & Crafts style, together with the colors of local earth and rock. Situated on a rise with distant views of the Pacific Ocean, the site invites a design that responds to its natural beauty. To link the house directly with its location, the house and landscape walls are made of native rock quarried from the site.

The approach to the house loops past the private outdoor areas into a courtyard edged by garages and covered loggias. Centered in the arrival court, a Southern live oak symbolically links the firm's Georgia roots and its new branches in California. Adjacent to the court, the guesthouse is detailed in board and batten siding with a corrugated tin roof. Its unpretentious materials allude to the thought of leaving the villa for a weekend in the country and visiting a secluded spa with views of the Pacific.

The house proper flows from the entry foyer in each direction toward the views of the distant ocean. The foyer contains a graceful stair and opens to the dining room and living room. Each of the formal rooms is detailed with earth-toned plaster walls and carefully detailed smooth stone walls with chiseled diamond-patterned edges. The formality of the living room develops from its molded and stenciled beamed ceiling carefully crafted from Lyptus wood that is limed and waxed to produce its subtle coloration. Similarly treated Lyptus is used for the high wainscoted paneling and the beamed ceiling in the dining room. Lyptus is a fast growing Earth-friendly eucalyptus that is harvested in sustainable forests in Brazil thus helping protect the rainforests.

From the foyer, the cross axis leads to the open flow of kitchen, breakfast room, and family room. These spaces open through large-paned windows and doors to walkways and the outdoor dining pavilion. Detailed with heavy timber constructions, the pavilion is positioned to maximize views of the swimming pool, ocean, and surrounding Santa Ynez Mountains. Lower-level entertainment spaces include the media area, game room, wine room, sauna, and yoga room.

Previous pages
  Arrival court with view toward dining room and main entry
Opposite
  Segmental stone arch capped with roof tiles marks the entrance
  to the arrival court
1 Site plan

1

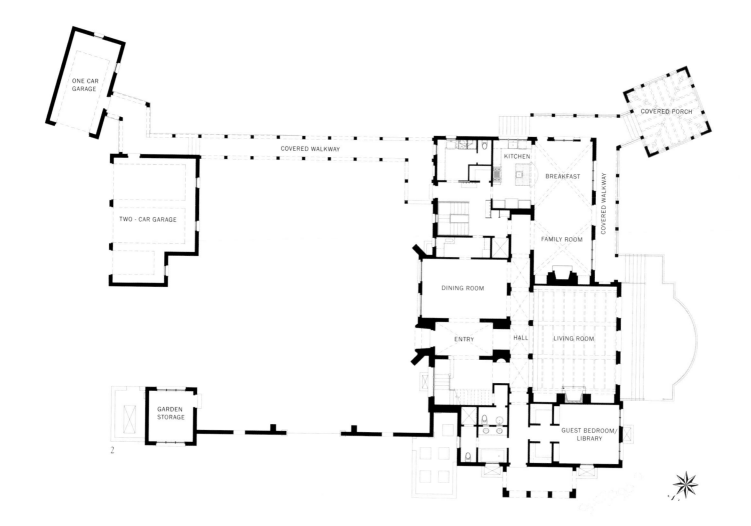

ONE CAR
GARAGE

COVERED WALKWAY

TWO - CAR GARAGE

KITCHEN

BREAKFAST

FAMILY ROOM

COVERED WALKWAY

COVERED PORCH

DINING ROOM

GARDEN
STORAGE

2

ENTRY

HALL

LIVING ROOM

GUEST BEDROOM/
LIBRARY

2   Main floor plan
3   Dining room
4   Living room
5   Detail of coffered ceiling
6   Coffered ceiling with stenciling
7   Living room

3

4

5

6

7

8

8   Family room
9   Breakfast room unites the family room and kitchen
10 Sauna flows into the yoga meditation room
11 Wine tasting room separated by glass wall from the
    temperature-controlled wine cellar
12 Kitchen seen from the breakfast room

9

10

11

12

13

14

15

13 Guest house bedroom opens to the arched ceiling of the living room beyond
14 Guest house kitchen
15 Guest house seen from the main house
16 Guest house living room with arched cedar shake ceiling

16

17 Beamed covered porch projecting from the kitchen/breakfast room
18 View from the arrival drive loop
Opposite
    The full height of the three-story house is seen only from the pool level

17

18

Hawn Residence
Atlanta, Georgia, 2002

An estate home of formal grandeur, this residence recalls 1920s-era Atlanta, a period when the city's foremost families provided their homes with opulent public façades that could be enjoyed by all. Following Beaux-Arts design principles, the five-bay façade reaches a crescendo in the center with the giant order columned temple. The craftsmanship of sculpted limestone walls and trim is especially evident in the 27-foot Corinthian columns. Taking three years to quarry and sculpt in Indiana, they are the largest monolithic limestone columns in the city. The entry surround displays a composition of Italian Mannerist detailing with broken pediment, swags, cartouche, and strapwork over fluted Doric columns. The garden façade is inspired by 18th-century Neo-Palladian work in England.

The interior rooms are aligned in a formal layout with the entry axis terminating in the two-story salon. From the circular entry hall another cross axis connects the dining room with the library. The double cube height of the library with its walnut and iron circular stair is inspired by George Vanderbilt's Art Library in Biltmore House in Asheville, North Carolina. Jacques Brunet of Paris, former head of the French Iron Workers' Guild, designed the wrought iron and bronze openwork and handrails throughout the interior and exterior of the home. His most dramatic work occurs in the majestic stair balustrade composed of gilded birds, cherubs, and floral motifs. All entertainment spaces are accessed from the terrace level and include a billiard room and pub, wine cellar and tasting room, home theater, shooting gallery, and an outdoor swimming pool.

Previous pages
   Close view of the arrival façade reveals the excellence of the Indiana
   limestone detailing
Opposite
   Main entry surround detailed with strapwork over fluted Doric columns
   that support a broken pediment with cartouche and swags; the 12-foot
   walnut doors are of 18th-century French origin
1   Site plan

1

2

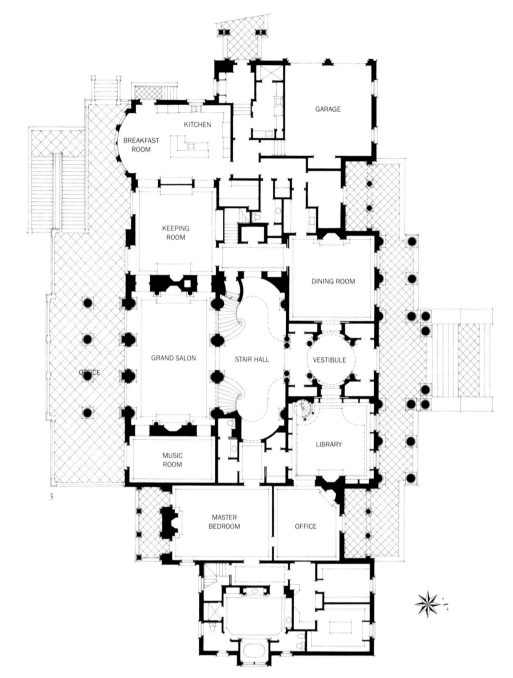

2 Detail of limestone swag below second-story windows
3 Main floor plan
4 Wrought iron railing created by Jacques Brunet of Paris
5 Entry column bases
Opposite
    View from stair hall into entry vestibule through solid Rouge de Roi columns with gilded Ionic capitals

GARAGE

KITCHEN

BREAKFAST ROOM

KEEPING ROOM

OFFICE

GRAND SALON

STAIR HALL

VESTIBULE

DINING ROOM

LIBRARY

MUSIC ROOM

3

MASTER BEDROOM

OFFICE

4

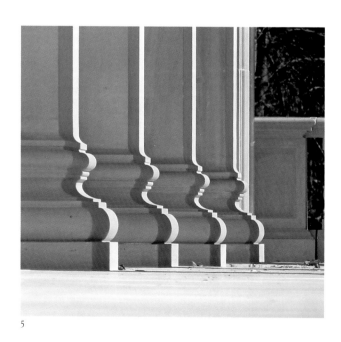

5

7

8

9

7 Circular vestibule opens to the elegant dining room
8 Double-story stair hall is accented with columns of Siena marble with gilded Corinthian capitals, iron railings by Jacques Brunet, and a slightly vaulted ceiling

9 Dining room with twin fluted Corinthian columns and an antique fireplace surround from Italy
10 Double-story grand salon with matched chimney pieces on facing end walls

10

11

12

11   Detail of the antique fireplace front that was enlarged to fit the scale of the room

12   Detail of coffered ceiling in the music room

13   Design of walnut and iron circular stair inspired by Richard Morris Hunt's Biltmore House in Asheville

Opposite
Double cube proportions of the library create a dramatic space with the fireplace wall as its focus

13

15

16

17

18

19

15 Kitchen
16 Wine tasting cellar
17 Family room toward grand salon
18 Master bath vanity
19 Master bath detailed in walnut
20 Master bedroom with walnut detailing and silk brocade-covered walls

20

21   Detail drawing of the hooded limestone fireplace
     surrounds

22   Triple arched doors of hand-wrought iron with
     bronze details designed by the late Jacques
     Brunet of Paris. A gate in France commissioned
     by Napoleon inspired Brunet's design.

23   Fireplace surround on the terrace level

Opposite
    Rear façade inspired by 16th-century Italian
    architect Andrea Palladio brought forward to the
    present with shaped pool opening to covered
    terrace. From the terrace one accesses the
    entertainment level including billiard room and
    pub, wine cellar and tasting room, home theater,
    and shooting gallery.

21

22

23

Paces End Estate
Atlanta, Georgia, 2001

Poised high above the Chattahoochee River, the family estate nestles into the natural beauty of its varied terrain. The site suggested architecture of subdued formality; the work of British architect Sir Edwin Lutyens and the Philadelphia firm of Mellor & Meigs were sources of inspiration. The approach to the house winds through a seemingly untouched pine and oak forest. With cleft-faced Indiana limestone, Vermont slate roof and mahogany door and window trim, the building mirrors the native colors of its surroundings. The arrival court is placed unpretentiously below the crest of the hill and the house's asymmetrical massing creates the image of an estate that has grown over time. The magnitude of the country manor cannot be gained from any single view. A colonnaded trellis leading past a lap pool to a screened garden house breaks the extent of the garden façade. Views to the river below are gained from formal terraces and planted pathways leading to a second garden house.

The interiors mirror the significance of natural materials already evident on the exterior of the house. Plain stucco walls are accented with smooth or rough limestone trim and floors vary from wide heart-pine boards to antique French terra cotta tile. The scale of rooms varies from intimate to grand. The projecting octagonal shape of the garden room accents the entry façade and is accessed immediately from the foyer. This delightful room, inspired by the grand Winter Garden at the Biltmore House in Asheville, visually opens upward with a glass ceiling suspended between mahogany trusses and outward through mahogany French doors. The heart of the home is shaped like a medieval hall with clerestory windows, heavy timber trusses, and a massive fireplace with a squared-timber mantle supported on stone corbels.

Previous pages
   View of the main façade dramatically
   emerges from the forested entry drive
Opposite
   The reserved character of the exterior
   continues in the cross-vaulted entry hall
1   Site plan

1

2 Main floor plan
3 Kitchen and vaulted family room
4 Grand salon
Opposite
  Grand salon opens to the dining room

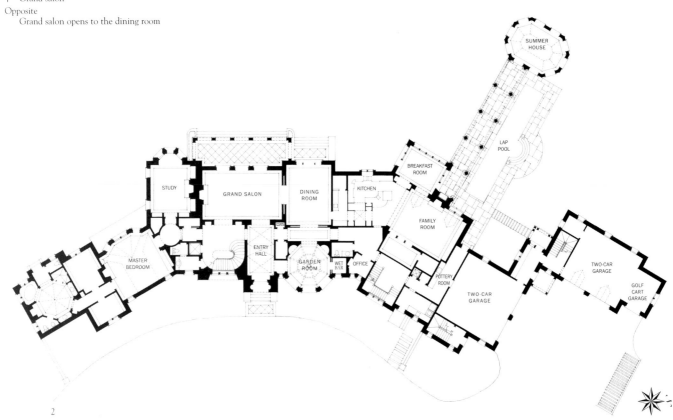

2

3

4

6   Detailed sections and reflected ceiling plan of the garden room
7   Octagonal garden room inspired by the Winter Garden at the
     Biltmore House in Asheville

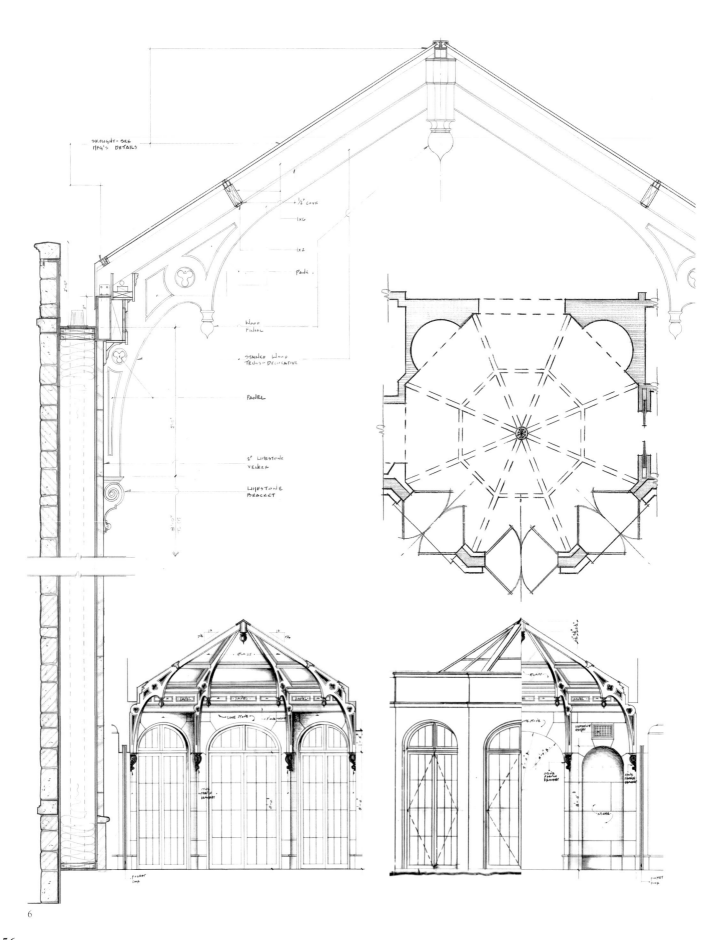

6

8

9

10

11

8   Garden path
9   Garden fountain at entry
10 Garden house
11 Peaked interior of the garden house
12 Trellised lap pool toward summer house
13 View from lap pool to the family room
14 View of the grand salon terrace

12

13

14

Georgian Residence
Atlanta, Georgia, 2003

Sited at the crest of a heavily wooded hill, the house is approached from a curving drive that terminates in a circular court. The formal, five-part Georgian design conveys the appearance of a characteristic sequence of American homes: the main house was built first, outbuildings were added later, and over time they were connected to the main house with enclosed passageways. This created history is conveyed through the detailing. All walls are made of fine Flemish bond brickwork, but the major block is detailed in limestone and the outbuildings are accented with simpler brick quoins. The entry is finely detailed in Indiana limestone including Doric columns that support a curving entablature and fluted Ionic pilasters that frame the mahogany entry door.

From the curving porch, one enters into a circular domed rotunda with a graceful stair ascending to an open gallery above. From this point one can circulate to the dining room or continue on axis to the living room and gardens beyond. The formal dining room has a developed cornice and broken pediment over doors and a fireplace surround of carved marble. The living room has a cornice with modillions and a noteworthy mantle that reproduces the Coade stone parlor mantle of the Tayloe (Octagon) House of 1798 in Washington, D.C. designed by Dr. William Thornton, original architect of the U.S. Capitol. The elegant study, with its Federal-style mantle and egg-and-dart cornice with dentil band, is made of American white pine resawn from 150-year-old timbers salvaged from demolished buildings.

The five-part garden façade looks over the formal garden and pool. Doric pilasters supporting an entablature divide the three sets of paired doors. By placing the covered porches to either side, the living room within has a high level of light and an immediate visual connection with the formal garden and pool.

Previous pages
   The exquisite detailing of Flemish bond brickwork and limestone details are apparent upon reaching the elevated arrival court
Opposite
   The semicircular porch is detailed entirely with Indiana limestone
1   Site plan

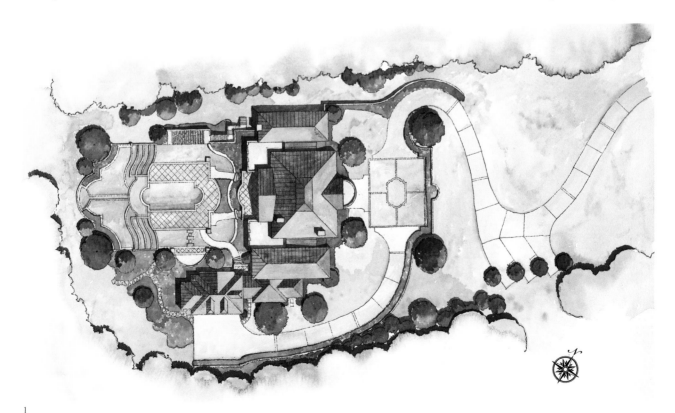

1

2   Main floor plan
3   The gallery opens through arches on piers into the living room;
     the fireplace surround reproduces the Coade stone parlor mantel
     of the Tayloe (Octagon) House of 1798 in Washington, D.C.
     designed by Dr. William Thornton
4   Circular entry rotunda
Opposite
     The two-story entry rotunda is capped with a low dome supported
     by delicate fluted Ionic columns.

2

3

4

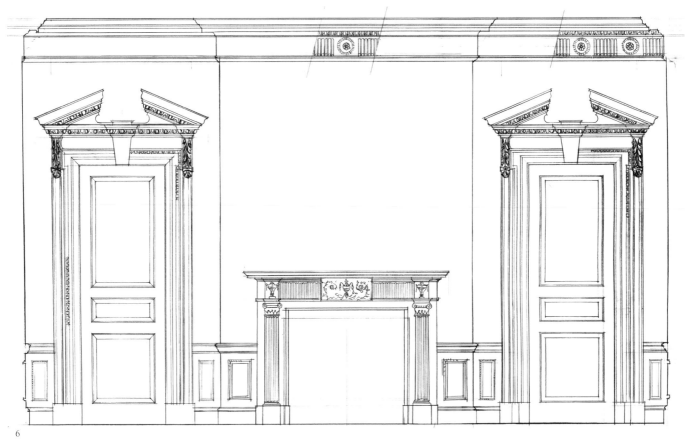

6

7

66

6   Detail drawing of the dining room with balanced doors topped with broken
    pediments
7   Dining room
8   Library detailed with American white pine resawn from 150-year-old timbers
    salvaged from demolished buildings
Following pages
    The balanced rear elevation seen from across the fountain and pool

8

Riddle Beach Retreat
Sea Island, Georgia, 2001

The brilliant sun of Italy suggested the appropriate solution for this site located on a barrier island on the edge of a ruggedly natural pine and palmetto forest. Views of the unpretentious formality of an Italian country villa welcome the visitor at the arrival court. At the clients' request, the general massing of the home draws upon Philip Shutze's Michael House in Macon, his last Baroque house design. The plain stuccoed walls are relieved with projected string courses, inset balusters, and a raised pediment—all detailed in Indiana limestone. The design balances an easy formality with complete connectedness to the delight of seaside existence.

Orienting the site toward the ocean required that the house be situated with the length facing the street. The typical plan aligns the entry on axis with the principal view, but in this house the architects introduce a strong cross-axis that redirects attention upon entering. A floating stair within a two-story space greets the visitor at the entrance and a flood of light and views of the ocean draws one toward the great room. The clients preferred both historic architecture and tall open spaces; the design responds with a contemporary feeling achieved through historic forms. The principal rooms were conceived as an open-air market that had at some later time been enclosed. Arches on piers supporting a 13-foot beamed ceiling define and separate the kitchen, foyer, and great room. The great room is a cool, bright space with white walls and matched classical fireplace surrounds made of limestone.

A five-bay Palladian-inspired façade faces the ocean with what appears to be a continuous second-story balcony. To maximize the light falling through the 12-foot arched windows into the great room, the floor of the center three bays is omitted to allow brilliant light to filter into the home's most important room. The side balconies provide ocean views for the master and guest bedrooms. All of the rooms convey the brightness of white walls and large windows; none more so than the kitchen with its spacious plan, arched window, and cabinetry discreetly tucked into the walls.

Previous pages
    The arrival façade projects images of the Italian Baroque with stucco walls and tile roofs
Opposite
    The entry hall connects all major rooms
1   Site plan

1

2   Main floor plan
3   Glimpse of great room gained from
     stair hall
Opposite
     Dining area centered in great room

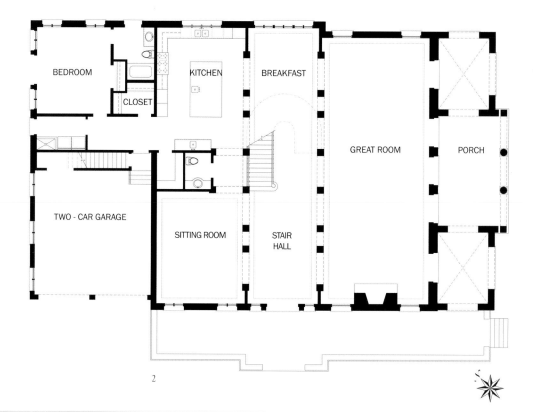

BEDROOM

CLOSET

KITCHEN

BREAKFAST

GREAT ROOM

PORCH

TWO - CAR GARAGE

SITTING ROOM

STAIR
HALL

2

3

5   Limited use of wall cabinets enhances spaciousness of kitchen
6   Breakfast room at end of stair hall beneath open stair
7   Master bath
8   Master bedroom
Following pages
    Ocean façade with two-story pedimented center inspired by the villas of
    Andrea Palladio; floors behind side balustrades are eliminated to provide
    increased light level in the great room

5

6

7

8

English Manor
Atlanta, Georgia, 2002

Set well back from the street, the house is approached by a lengthy winding drive through manicured woodland. The choice of English manor-style forms in rough stone accented with carved limestone details conveys the balanced, but not formal, character of the house. The strength of Tennessee fieldstone walls and multicolored weathering slate roofs communicates that the domain of such a family lies beyond. Rather than numerous formal rooms, the client requested a design connected directly to the outdoors and linked by a variety of entertainment spaces.

The kitchen and eating spaces compose the physical center of the house. The breakfast room, dining room, and keeping room revolve around this center. Subtle detailing of the walls increases the sense of massiveness, especially in the inset window of the breakfast room. Here, the architects used a single sheet of glass with no divisions so the room connects directly to the gardens beyond.

The keeping room and billiard room have walls and heavy timber trusses made from reclaimed teak. The dark tone of the rooms contrasts with the brilliant light pouring through the projecting wall of doors and windows. The elongated octagonal plan of the billiard room is capped by a 16-foot-tall ceiling covered in heavy planking and timber frames. These entertainment spaces link to the swimming pool and stone cabana, completing the casual elegance of the entire ensemble. Adjacent to the second-floor master suite, a round screen porch topped by a tapered turret roof provides a view over the gardens and pool.

Previous pages
    First view of the main façade from the curving entry drive
Opposite
    View of the entry façade
1   Site plan

1

2 Main floor plan
3 From the porte-cochère, the private entry leads through the mud room into the keeping room
4 The rear elevation looking toward the variously shaped rooms including the billiard room, kitchen, and the porch turret
5 Main entry stair

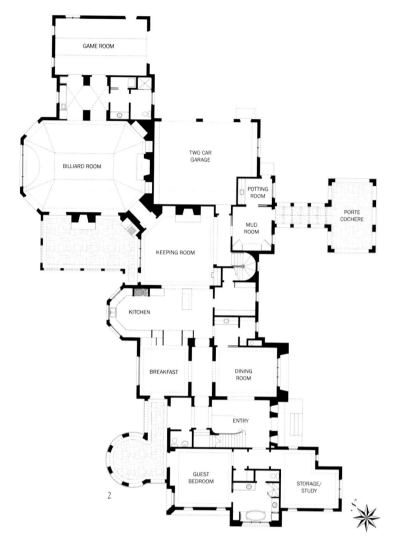

GAME ROOM

BILLIARD ROOM

TWO CAR GARAGE

POTTING ROOM

PORTE COCHERE

MUD ROOM

KEEPING ROOM

KITCHEN

BREAKFAST

DINING ROOM

ENTRY

GUEST BEDROOM

STORAGE/ STUDY

2

3

4

5

6 The large undivided window visually connects the breakfast room with the gardens beyond
7 The vaulted billiard room is detailed with walls and trusses of reclaimed teak
8 The potting room opens to the mud room
9 The playful game room fits within a barn-shaped space

6

7

8

9

10 Faceted entry door surround with cable molding
11 Entry door surround detail
12 Stone and slate roof detail
13 Garden wall detail of Tennessee fieldstone
14 Rear elevation looking across the pool to the billiard room and turreted porch beyond

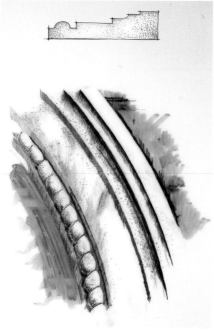

11

10

12

13

14

Hacienda Hermosa
Montecito, California, 2006

Through a careful renovation, this modestly interesting 1980s house on a dramatic site emerged as a convincingly detailed Spanish-style home. The essential elements of door and window openings and room locations remained untouched, but finer materials improved the quality of the design. At the main entrance, the grooved stucco door surround was replaced with an arched, carved limestone surround with a molded edge and an extended keystone. The painted doors on the first and second floors were replaced with natural mahogany. New iron lanterns and an iron balcony railing based on the abstract image of the Ionic volute replaced the former undetailed pickets.

On the garden side, the curving tower was opened with new windows to take better advantage of the dramatic views of the Pacific. In the interior, the simple round room took an octagonal shape with walls of classically detailed pilasters, wooden inset shelves, and a beamed peaked ceiling, becoming a dramatic new office library. Also on the garden side, all doors were replaced with mahogany and glass double panels, and copper downspouts and mahogany pickets replaced the same items of lesser materials.

Although the room locations remained unchanged, the interiors were basically gutted. Remaining items such as roof beams and trusses were stripped of paint or smoothed from their rough-sawn state to become elegant architectural elements. Simple plaster fireplace surrounds were replaced with those of classically detailed cast stone. The most dramatic addition was the curving stair with cast-stone treads and iron and brass railing, a concept developed from a study of the Santa Barbara designs of the architect George Washington Smith.

The house is sited within lush gardens to take advantage of the views of the Pacific Ocean. A new pool and Jacuzzi cascade down the hill from an axial alignment with the house's great room.

Previous pages
    Rear façade opening to terraces and fountain
Opposite
    Main entrance with new door surround and ironwork
1   Site plan

1

2   Main floor plan
3   Main entrance from the arrival court
4   Main entrance detail looking through
    to the Pacific Ocean
Opposite
    Main stair rising in the dining room

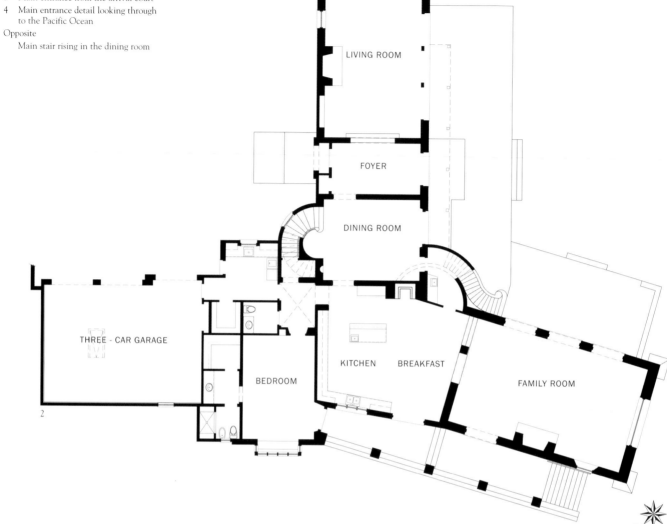

LIVING ROOM

FOYER

DINING ROOM

THREE - CAR GARAGE

BEDROOM

KITCHEN   BREAKFAST

FAMILY ROOM

2

3

4

6　View from the living room to the entry hall
7　The family room connects through arched openings to the breakfast room
8　Heavy timber ceiling connects the living room with similar details in the entry hall
9　Heavy timber trusses accent the family room

6

7

8

9

10 Breakfast room and kitchen
11 View from kitchen toward dining room
12 View from kitchen toward family room

11

12

14

13

13   Section detail of office
14   Octagonal office
15   Pool and spa seen from the terrace with view toward the ocean
16   Rear façade looking toward living room

15

16

Cohen Lake Retreat
Lake Burton, Georgia, 2000

Sited in woods above an expansive North Georgia lake, this house was designed with a desire to fit comfortably within the natural setting. The variety of masses and the natural materials of wood shingles and rough native stone walls connect the house with earlier American Arts & Crafts and Queen Anne styles. The difficulty often presented by these styles is balancing asymmetry. Here the balance is achieved with boldly overlapping and intersecting gambrel roofs, a low single-story wing, and a projecting turret roof.

The interior continues the interplay of rough with refined. The axis leading from the covered entry passes through a gallery of open segmental arches supported on highly refined Doric piers and terminates at a vast wall-sized Palladian window. From this vantage point, views of the sweeping lakefront focus on the shingled boathouse perched on a high stone base. Also reflecting the spirit of the location, the master bedroom invites nature indoors with its most unusual structural white birch log-trussed ceiling and beaded paneled walls.

A nautical theme generated by the clients' love of sailing produced inspired solutions for detailing throughout the house. At the entry stair and second floor balcony overlooking the living room, the upper handrail is detailed in wood with the appearance of the swinging curves of woven rope. At the newel post it takes on the additional illusion of a looped and tied knot. The octagonal turreted room seen from the entry has the aspect of the captain's bridge with commanding views of the lake and a floor detailed as a compass rose in Brazilian cherry, quarter-sawn white ash, and black walnut.

Previous pages
    Entry façade from the arrival court
Opposite
    The repeating gambrel roofs of the main and boat houses can best be appreciated from the lake
1   Site plan

1

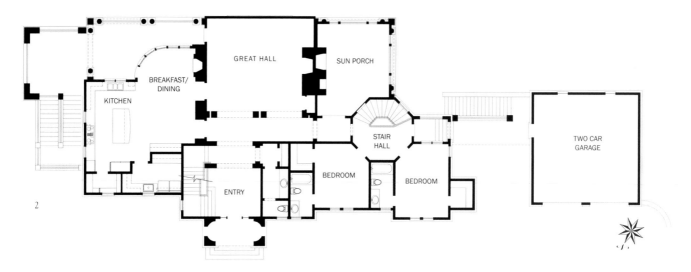

2 Main floor plan
3 Balcony bridging across entry foyer
4 Knotted handrail detailed in wood
5 Newel post and wooden rope handrail
6 Great hall and stair newel millwork detail
Opposite
    The double height great hall with hammerbeam
    trusses and river rock fireplace surround

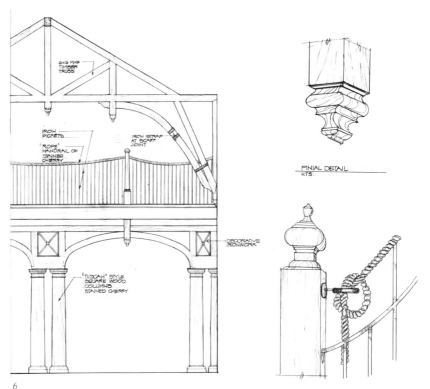

8 Kitchen with stacked stone range surround and reclaimed wood beams
9 Master bedroom with structural white birch log-trussed ceiling
10 Sun porch with fireplace surround detailed in stone and sheets of bark

9

10

Opposite

Heavy timber detailing of the family room

12 Ground level loggia and spa waterfall

13 Ironwork spider web gate

14 Lake elevation

12

13

14

All'Ombra
Atlanta, Georgia, 2000

Sheltered on a hill surrounded by hardwood forest and a tumbling mountain stream, the client replaced her childhood home with one appropriate to her adult life. The personal connection with the site and the addition of materials representing memories of far-flung travel resulted in a unique eclectic design. The body of the house is conceived as a bridge supported by symmetrical entry masses that symbolize a balanced life of family and friends. Through the left arched cherry door one gains access to the connected kitchen–family area; through the right, one enters a formal foyer with travertine floors and the glassy surfaces of Venetian plaster walls. The exterior provides the first evidence that the style of the house is not easily categorized. Stuccoed walls, iron-railed balconies and the clay-tiled roof create an Italian character. An Asian aspect is reflected in the brass rain cups that replace traditional downspouts, allowing the rain to playfully splash from the roof to the ground.

The vaulted 22-foot-tall cubic living room continues the Italian character of the exterior. The Italianate references are seen in the reserved white plaster walls and a window organization of circles and arches inspired by Palladio's Villa Poiana. Reclaimed cherry floors provide a warm tone. The formal room's principal ornament is the stone fireplace surround. The Mannerist design with stretched classical consoles includes images of the site's native creatures so beloved by the client—an owl, beaver, fox, snake, birds, and turtles.

The significance of family is apparent throughout the serious, yet playful design. The live-in kitchen area opens to an arcaded side porch with a raised hearth and fireplace. The exterior wall is ornamented with open-mouthed dolphins that serve as rain spouts for the terrace above. A trellis supports the growth of rose, wisteria, muscadine, and jasmine that give the outdoor family room sweet scents and dramatic seasonal color.

The family's world travels are symbolically present in the ornamental dragons that guard the entry gate and family room. Considered an emblem of good fortune by the Chinese, the dragon motif appears in the carved stone bases that support tapered teak columns from China. The fireplace surround in carved flint stone, also from China, depicts two dragons throwing a ball. The overall concept of these details is a fusion of east and west, producing an image similar to an early Greek temple with an Asian influence. Bronze and copper dragons landing with lanterns in their mouths ornament the estate's stone entry gates.

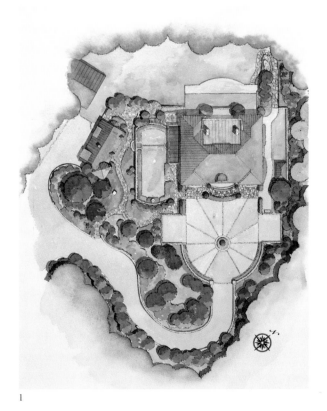

Previous pages
  Main elevation from the arrival court
Opposite
  Entrance to the kitchen/family area
1 Site plan

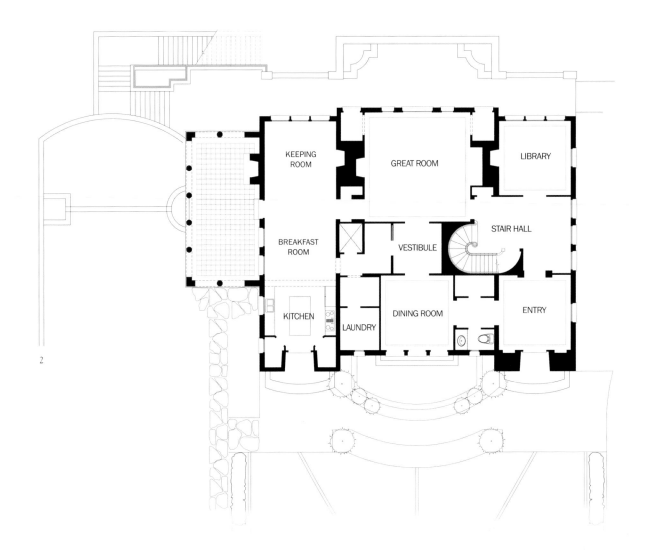

2   Main floor plan
3   Conceptual front elevation sketch
Opposite
    Entry to the formal side of the house

3

5 The great room with its window wall inspired by Andrea Palladio's Villa Poiana
6 Dining room toward arched windows
7 Detail showing creatures native to the site
8 Dining room opening to the great room

6

7

8

9   Kitchen looking toward the informal entry door
10 View of the kitchen from the breakfast area
11 Master bedroom
12 Master bathroom
13 Terrace level fireplace with Chinese dragon details

9

10

11

12

13

14   Stream cascade adjacent to entry drive
15   Entry dragon gate detail
16   Arrival court with view of dragon gates
17   Garden waterfall
18   Loggia accessed from the breakfast room

14

15

16

17

Spring Hill Farm
McLean, Virginia, 2005

The site is located in Virginia, at the border with Maryland, in an area marked by the strong local building traditions of its 18th-century German settlers. Constructed of local stone with plain functional detailing and no extraneous ornamentation, these German farmers' houses reflected a conservative spirit of living with the land. Inspired by this unique architectural context, the design of Spring Hill Farm needed to be more than its simple four-room neighbors. The architects developed a fictional history for the house to direct their creation of the appearance of growth by addition. As needs for space changed over the generations of its owners, new rooms were added. The main house in stone connects to a number of whitewashed additions spread horizontally across its face. The extent of the house's size is hidden though the U-shaped plan that wraps the master suite and family wing around an interior garden.

The detailing is consistently simple like its neighbors, but it maintains an underlying sophistication. In keeping with its context, the "historic" house is built of stone—not the local fieldstone, but a carefully selected range of color and texture from quarries in Virginia, Maryland, and Pennsylvania. The "later" additions are built of smaller materials that are whitewashed as would also have occurred in historic additions. The detailing is fundamental and without overt elegance: the roofs are slate, columns are squared with chamfered edges, and the window sills and lintels are solid slabs of stone or low segmental stone arches.

In an unusual move for an imposing design, the main entrance sequence occurs under the shed porch directly into the living room. This arrangement relates specifically to the concept of the area's historic houses. The living room has a beamed ceiling and fireplace, but it opens in each direction through pairs of lighted French doors. The theme of history continues through the house in the use of reclaimed timbers in the peaked ceilings of the main rooms.

Previous page
    Main elevation from the arrival court
Opposite
    Garage and water pump fit comfortably with the surrounding
    18th-century farmhouses
1   Site plan

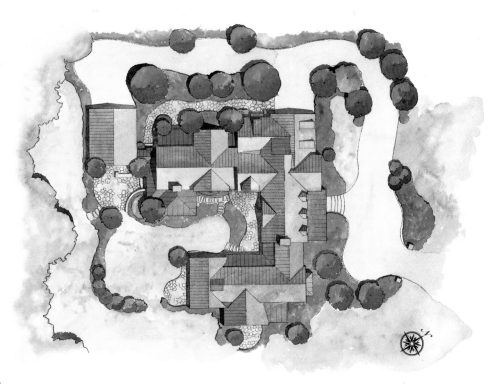

1

2

2   Porch and wall dormer partial elevation
3   Main entry under covered porch leads directly to the living room in the style
    of the historic houses in the area

3

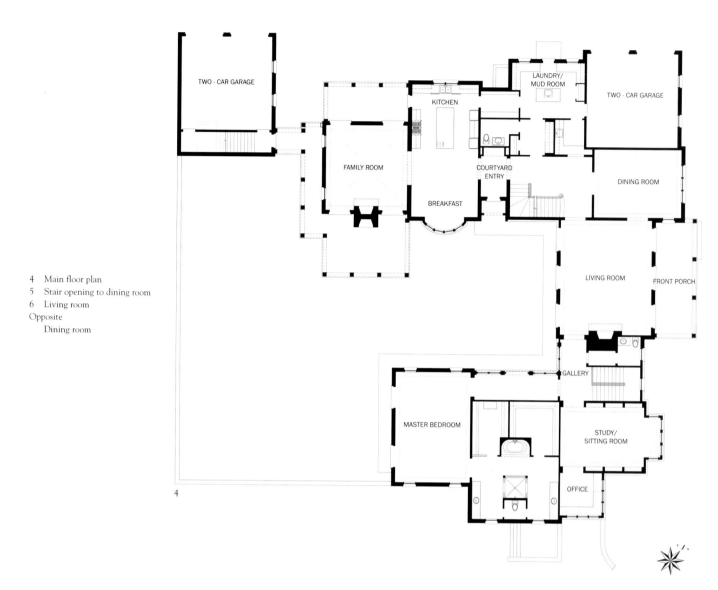

4   Main floor plan
5   Stair opening to dining room
6   Living room
Opposite
    Dining room

4

5

6

8

9

8   Kitchen
9   Breakfast room
10   Family room
11   Family room fireplace
12   Study
13   Wine cellar tasting room

10

11

12

13

14

15

16

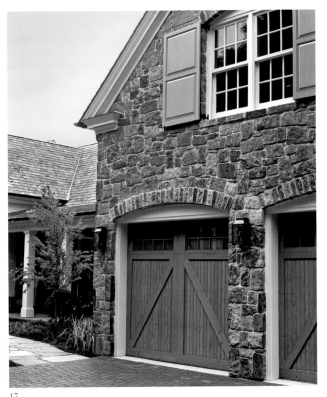

14 Master bedroom
15 Master bathroom
16 Patio opening from master bedroom
17 Garage
18 Auto court and kitchen garden

17

18

Echols Residence
Atlanta, Georgia, 2005

The clients presented an interesting challenge: to adapt the appearance of a much-admired historic façade onto a spatially modern floor plan and accomplish all of this in the setting of an especially difficult narrow lot. The historic house—the Willis Jones House—had its own peripatetic story. It originally sat above Peachtree Street on the edge of Brookwood Hills and was disassembled and moved to its current site on West Paces Ferry and Moores Mill Road, now located on a new flat site. The details of the elegant historic composition were closely quoted in Flemish bond brick and cast-stone elements. As the new stone detailing ages and darkens, the relationship between the two buildings will grow more evident.

Beyond the historically composed façade, a series of elegant formal spaces are linked by axes. Immediately upon entering, the visitor is greeted by an intriguing 20-foot-tall foyer with second-story lighting. A cross axis connects the study and dining room with the axis terminating on the centered fireplaces. Proceeding from the foyer, the visitor next encounters the gently spiraling stair contained within an oval-shaped room completed by a smooth low dome above. The rising stair hall leads to the refined formal great room whose brilliant lighting is achieved with triple tall-arched double doors.

The master suite is located on the main level with four guest suites on the second floor. On the terrace level, the billiard room, exercise spa and sauna, and wine-tasting room and cellar open to the pool terrace beyond. The wine-tasting room is situated below the graceful spiral stair at the entry, recalling the curving walls of the oval room on each floor.

Previous pages
    Main elevation with giant order Corinthian pilasters
Opposite
    Double-height entry hall lighted by second-floor window
1   Site plan

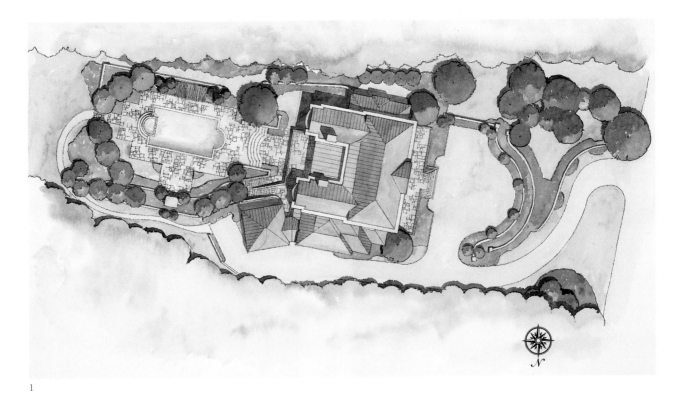

1

2 Main floor plan
3 Study with paneled walls and
   coffered ceiling of matching mahogany
4 Great room mantle detail
Opposite
   Great room

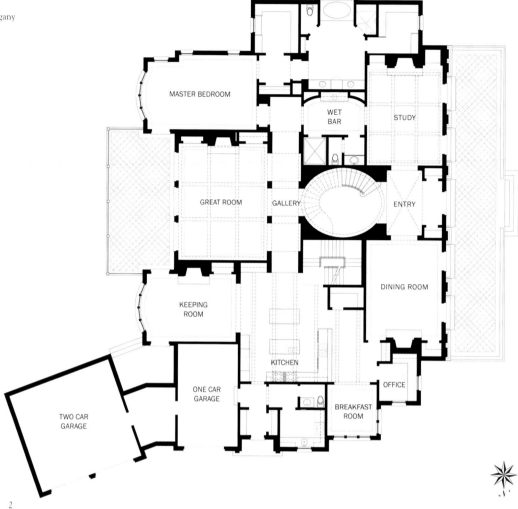

MASTER BEDROOM

WET BAR

STUDY

GREAT ROOM

GALLERY

ENTRY

KEEPING ROOM

DINING ROOM

KITCHEN

OFFICE

ONE CAR GARAGE

BREAKFAST ROOM

TWO CAR GARAGE

2

3

4

6 Wet bar with mahogany cabinetry and curved wall details
7 Kitchen
8 Wine cellar and tasting room

6

7

9 Outdoor fireplace and seating area adjacent to the pool
10 Rear elevation from the pool

9

10

Miller Residence
Atlanta, Georgia, 2002

The clients' interests in golf and gardening are intertwined on the site of their residence. The house sits on the edge of the golf course and a variety of developed gardens make a smooth transition between the two. The clients requested both an English reference and an unpretentious air for their design. The low-profile, story-and-a-half design prevents the house from dominating the site. The low wall and slight rise to the entrance create a subtle natural pedestal for the house. The clients' desires were further satisfied by the spirited asymmetrical design that recalls the 1920s Philadelphia suburban architecture of the celebrated architects Mellor & Meigs. Their characteristic use of fine materials coincides with the current architects' insistence on similar selections. The body of the home is made entirely of ashlar limestone with eaves and cornices of solid limestone. To further enhance the strength conveyed by stone walls, the entry and dining room window are recessed within extended walls, creating a sense of substance associated with massive masonry. The fine materials will age gracefully and enhance the timeless quality of the house.

From the covered arched entry porch, one enters beneath back-wrapping stairs. This sequence provides a warm, sheltered feeling followed by the relief of moving into a tall two-story space. The warmth of the wood-paneled walls characterizes the overall design. From the foyer one moves directly into the family room and catches a first glimpse of the gardens beyond. The desired lack of pretension is conveyed by the comfortable attitude of the calm-toned family room and the lack of a formal space signified as a living room. The importance of gardens views is accommodated by the choice of arched double French doors with steel muntins. The thin profile of the steel doors provides less visual obstruction than the more typical choice of thick wood muntins in similarly shaped doors. A constant connection to the lovely English-style gardens is made through the kitchen's bow window and the breakfast room's double French doors that open directly to the stone-walled herb garden.

Previous pages
  Arrival elevation
Opposite
  Main door beneath the back wrapping stair
1 Site plan

1

2 Main floor plan
3 Antique white pine study
Opposite
   Family room toward the garden

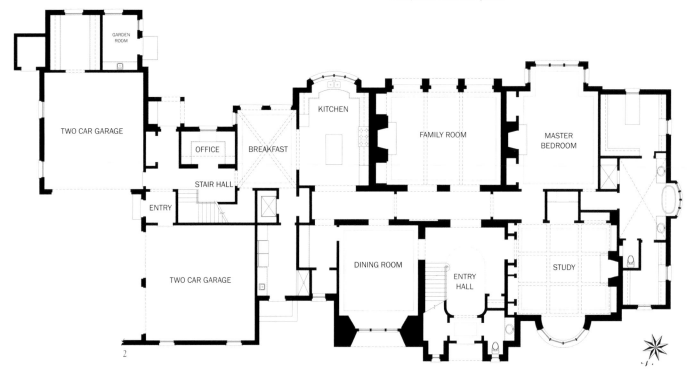

2

3

5

5   Master bedroom
6   Fireplace detail in master bedroom
7   Master bathroom

6

7

8   Rendering of garden room entrance
9   View of the garden from the family room terrace
10   Elevation view toward the master bedroom
11   Elevation view from the garden room toward
     the family room
12   Garden view from the family room to the
     breakfast room

9

8

154

10

11

12

Acheson Residence
Birmingham, Alabama, 2001

Views of surrounding mountains and a site of twin knolls divided by a slight ravine inspired the physical design of this home near Birmingham, Alabama. The upper arrival terrace leads to the entry by way of a walled garden enclosed on one side by a triple-arched loggia detailed with giant order columns and mullioned glazed windows. Like all the principal rooms, the foyer provides an axial view oriented to the mountains and spatially opens to the dining room. The arrival level includes all formal rooms plus the master suite with each room opening to overlook terraces with views of unspoiled forests.

The challenging sloping site accommodated space for the at-grade swimming pool, spa, and lower living room located just beneath the formal living room. The site also inspired a solution to reduce the visual impact of a five-car garage by accommodating a two-story building. With three cars below and two cars above, the garage's single-story profile on the arrival level harmonizes with the composition of the main building.

The home's architectural style reflects that of Florida's Addison Mizner and designs that influenced him from Spain and North Africa. The exterior walls are composed of rough textured stucco with a rusticated base made of buff-colored Indiana limestone. The flow of interior space is defined by changing floor patterns such as the foyer's limestone floor with marble latticework that leads to the dining room's limestone floor with wood inlay. The stylistic character determined by client and architect is conveyed in details such as the garden's hand-forged iron gates, and the unusual Moroccan-inspired dining room with its plaster walls and geometric patterns in the wood and leather ceiling. With its open truss ceiling of heart pine and iron and a carved coral stone fireplace surround, the living room completes the twin concepts of Mizner's Florida plus North African inspiration. The fireplace surround was inspired by one at Nuestro Paradiso, the Palm Beach home designed by Julius Jacobs in the 1920s.

Previous pages
    Arrival court with view of walled garden and attached garage
Opposite
    View of front façade
1   Site plan

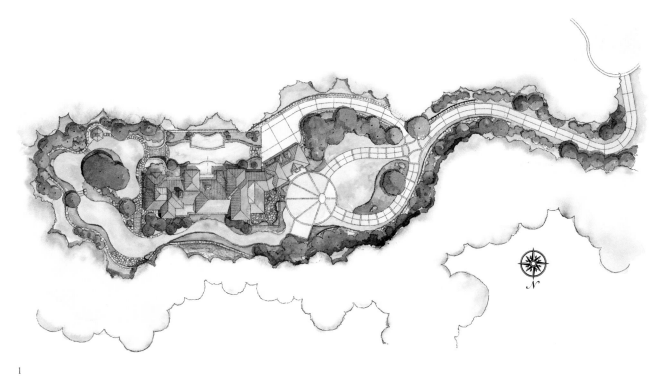

1

2 Main floor plan
3 Dining room window from the walled entry garden
Opposite
    Fountain and entry within the walled garden

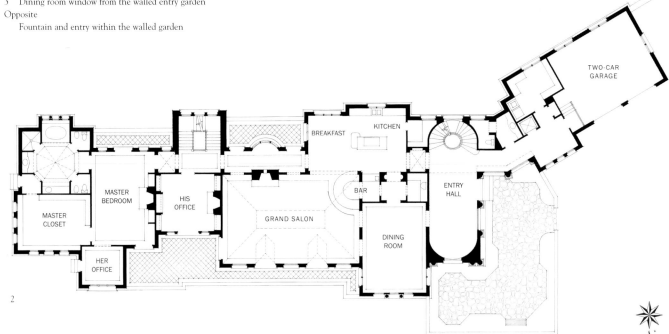

2

3

5   Elevation and details of the wrought iron entry gate
6   Entry to walled garden

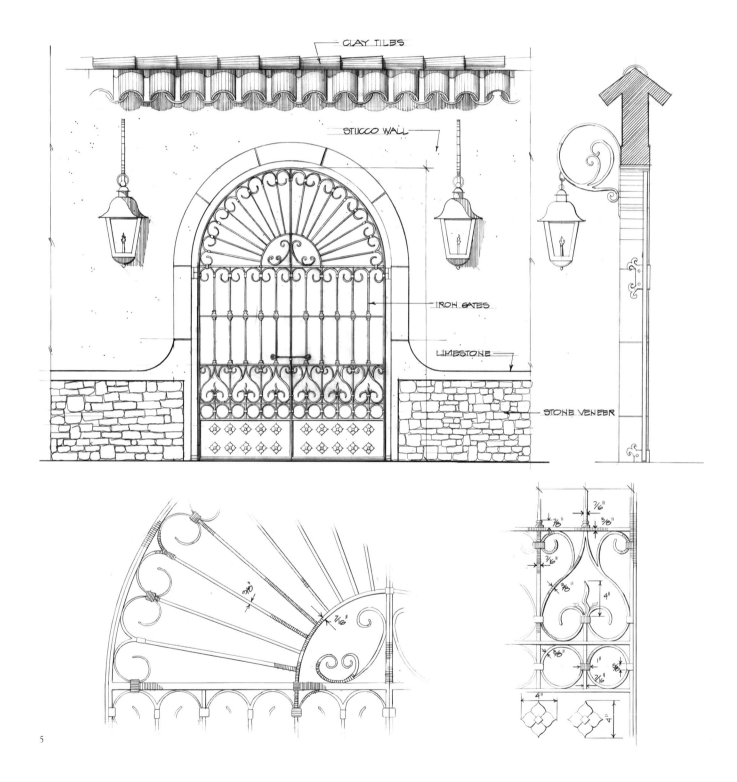

CLAY TILES

STUCCO WALL

IRON GATES

LIMESTONE

STONE VENEER

5

7 Entry hall toward the circular stair
8 Circular stair curving through three floors
9 Main entry toward the walled garden

8

9

10   Great room with openwork trussed ceiling
11   Moroccan-inspired dining room with wood and leather ceiling

10

12   Kitchen toward the entry hall
13   Master bathroom
14   Master bedroom

13

14

15   Lap pool located on-grade below the living room
Opposite
    View from the gazebo toward the rear elevation

15

Sturm Residence
Atlanta, Georgia, 2003

At the clients' request, the house was designed to reflect the historic character of an English Manor house. The architects combined several periods of English history into a new, but related evocation of history. The house sits on a high and imposing site and the strength of the material chosen gives an aura of permanence. The simple, but elegantly detailed walls are made of limestone quarried in Tennessee and Kentucky, combined to give a range of blue-gray and brown colors. The entry details are straightforward, with squared Indiana limestone sills and lintels and a simple stone arched entry surround. The notes of extra elegance are reserved for the private side of the house where the façade is more active with triple gables and side porches. Wooden pergolas supported on Doric limestone columns cover the twin porches. The center covered porch breaks with the solemnity of the house and its earlier English style by introducing the curving lines of a Regency period openwork iron and copper trellis.

The plan continues the English Manor concept with a central vestibule that includes a boot-warming fireplace of the type found in a traditional house in a cold and wet climate. The cross hall connects the four major public rooms. These rooms exhibit a range of expression, from the rough pine-beamed ceiling in the keeping room to the slightly curving ceiling of the elegant living room. The paneled sitting room is created from cypress logs recovered from the Sewanee River. During the timbering process in the 19th century, when logs were floated downriver to the planing mills, some logs sank to the bottom of the river. Many have recently been recovered and finally processed for their intended use.

Previous pages
    Arrival façade at the crest of the site
Opposite
    Entry door beneath the back wrap stair
1   Site plan

1

2 Main floor plan
3 Antique cypress library
Opposite
    Great room with low vaulted ceiling in the style of 18th-century British
    architect John Soane

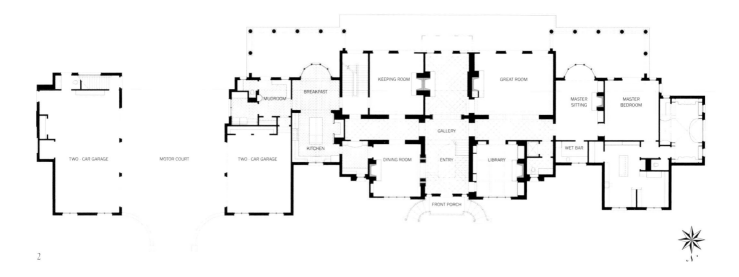

2

3

5   Breakfast room with sitting area in the bay window
6   Kitchen
7   Sitting room
8   Master bathroom
9   Master bedroom

5

6

7

8

9

10 Elevation of the iron and copper porch
11 Regency-style porch
12 Garage from the approach drive
13 Rear façade with wooden trellises balancing the center gabled mass

11

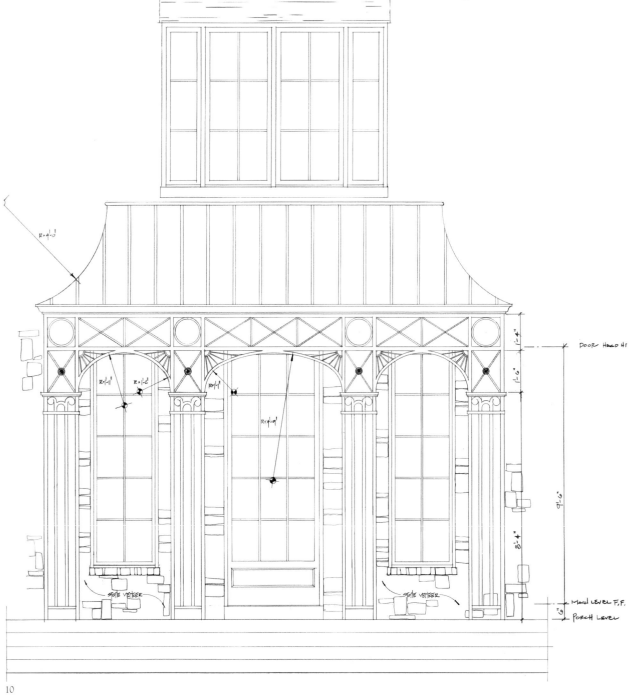

10

12

13

Cannon Residence
Atlanta, Georgia, 2003

The clients' interest in historic architecture and reserved contemporary spaces resulted in a design that seamlessly blends these two potentially divergent concepts. The five-part massing of the house reflects the influence of 16th-century Italian architect Andrea Palladio on later 18th- and 20th-century designers in Britain. From the centered entrance drive, the house appears like many historic designs, with a main block and twin side buildings connected by enclosed hyphens. Here however, the master suite is contained on one side and the kitchen on the opposite side.

The calm clarity of the planning is supported by the dignity of the building's construction materials. Suggestive of the work of Britain's Quinlan Terry, the walls and trim combine cut stone with finely cast stone elements. The architects selected a buff-toned Indiana limestone with a guillotine cut. For an added aged appearance the stone was tumbled and washed with acid to bring out colorful impurities.

The contemporary character is immediately apparent upon entering the circular domed foyer. This space, as all the others, is highly detailed, but calm in its overall impression. The placement of the stairs in a separate location allows the foyer to smoothly connect the formal dining and living rooms, achieving the desired effect of smoothly flowing space. The cross-axis hall leads to closed walls of the master suite at one end, and at the other end it creates a sense of openness between the dining room and stair. The master suite includes a semi-private library connected on axis with the private sitting area—both are separated and yet connected by an inset pair of double doors.

The rear elevation forms an axis with the swimming pool and formal garden. The sense of calm develops from the biaxial symmetry of matched bow windows, covered loggias, and the two-story gabled mass. Particular lighting effects are achieved by pulling the loggias away from the centered living room, allowing direct light into the highly detailed interior while providing shaded cover and privacy for the master sitting room. The home as a whole conveys the clients' desire for the familiar design references of history with the calming effects of orderly interiors.

Previous pages
   The axial drive reveals the balanced harmony of the main façade
Opposite
   The domed entry hall is lighted by the Palladian window above the entry door
1   Site plan

2 Main floor plan
3 Gallery between living room and entry
4 Stair hall view from dining room
5 Dining room
6 Living room with deeply coffered ceiling supported on Ionic pilasters

MASTER
BEDROOM

SITTING
ROOM

LIBRARY

LIVING ROOM   GALLERY   ENTRY

DINING
ROOM

KEEPING
ROOM

KITCHEN

BREAKFAST
ROOM

FOUR CAR
GARAGE

OFFICE #2   OFFICE #1

2

3

4

5

6

Opposite
    Kitchen
8   Sitting room off master bedroom
9   Master bathroom
10 Master bedroom

8

9

10

Azalea House Renovation
Atlanta, Georgia, 1997 and 2001

The architects had a rare opportunity to twice renovate this home for two separate clients with different needs and demands. The original house was built in 1938 for the well-known developer, Charles H. Black, who created the residential area of Tuxedo, Valley, and Blackland roads at the center of Atlanta's Buckhead district. Charles H. Black kept this prized 3-acre site for himself and selected an English Manor-style stucco with half-timber detailing for his new home. By the 1990s the original Depression-era kitchen and other amenities in the house were inadequate for current use.

The first renovation demanded a major reorganization of a virtual rabbit warren of small rooms into larger, more useful spaces. Some rooms, such as the living and dining rooms, required little more than new moldings, while the master suite, for example, was created from the combined space of two original bedrooms. The original kitchen was entirely replaced with a new kitchen, breakfast room, and powder room. These spaces connected to the open-trussed ceiling of the great room, an original space in the house, but one that received significant changes with each owner.

The principal new additions extended the house into the grounds with a renovated pool cabana and a combined new guesthouse and three-car garage building. The nondescript 1970s-era pool cabana was brought into harmony with the half-timbered main house. The playful massing of the new guesthouse exists within the gabled slate roofs capping the significant garage created to house the client's antique car collection.

Previous pages
    The façade of the original 1938 house remains virtually unchanged
Opposite
    The new entry court with fountain
1   Site plan

1

2 Main floor plan
3 Dining room
Opposite
  Living room

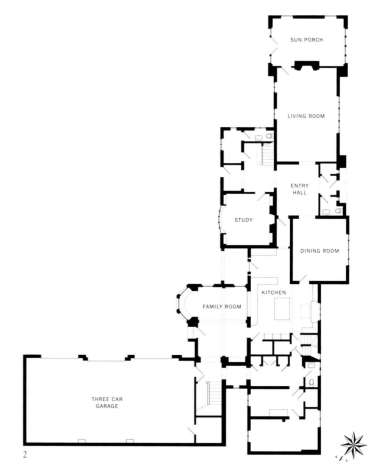

2

3

6

Opposite
  Renovated kitchen with hand-hewn ceiling beams
6 Breakfast room
7 Family room added entirely in the 2001 renovation
8 Kitchen

7

8

9 Gallery leading to media room
10 Media room
11 Study

9

10

12 Pool house before renovation
13 Pool house expansion plan
14 Pool house after expansion
Opposite
New carriage house

12

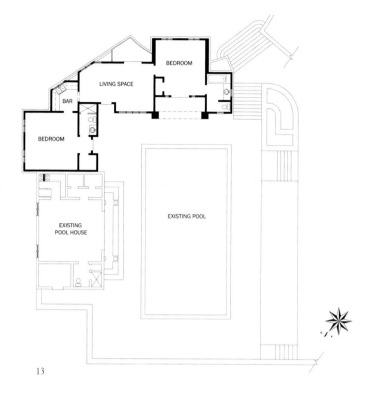

BEDROOM

LIVING SPACE

BAR

BEDROOM

EXISTING
POOL HOUSE

EXISTING POOL

13

14

West Paces Village Overview
Atlanta, Georgia, 1998 – 2002

The fourteen-home development on 14 acres was sensitively inserted into an area of Atlanta's most architecturally significant historic homes from the 1920s. The design carefully integrated thirteen new homes and restored and expanded an existing house by leaving the majority of the acreage undisturbed, allowing the 100-year-old trees to survive and shield the homes from existing street views. More than half the development (8.4 acres) was left as undisturbed green space. The innovative concept allowed the architects to create highly desirable homes whose overall sizes, however, were less than half the square footage of homes in the surrounding neighborhood. The result was homes nestled into mature forests rather than the standard for the day of enormous houses dwarfing their miniscule lots.

Previous pages
    Historic Richardson-Franklin House
Opposite
    Front gate
1   Entry gate and guardhouse

The principal curving road from West Paces Ferry replaces the original driveway to the Hugh Richardson estate that still exists on the ridge above the current development. The Harrison firm renovated this large estate house, designed originally by the New York architect Aymar Embury II, as well as the home for Richardson's son Hugh, Jr.

The new development was conceived as a neighborhood of homes stylistically in harmony with Hugh Richardson, Jr.'s original home, built in the 1930s. To accomplish the coherence of new and old, the architects developed each home with general references to the original Normandy-style historic home. Detail references included slate roofed round turrets, stone and stucco walls, and steeply peaked gable roofs, often mixed with the French-style slate hip roof. The resulting neighborhood is one of peaceful coexistence between historic architecture and its new neighbors that successfully maintains a balance between the built and the natural realms.

1

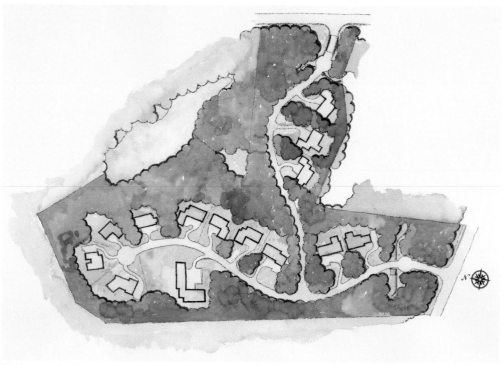

Development site plan

West Paces Village
Richardson-Franklin House Renovation, 2004

Additions to historic homes offer particular challenges to both architect and client, and a great deal can be interpreted about each in the process. This 1930s home designed by noted New York architect Aymar Embury II required preservation, restoration, and additional new space. Client and architect agreed to preserve the main arrival façade and to add needed expansion space off the rear of the house. This arrangement preserved the public view of the historic home and also provided additional private space in the area most protected from public view.

All significant details of the original house were studied and duplicated in the new work thus producing seamless additions. In years to come it will be difficult to determine where the original meets the modern additions. Such a respectful approach is not often applied in additions to historic work, a shortcoming that leads to unpleasant contrasts between new and old. The 1930s character of the home is evidenced in the simplified details like rope mouldings, linear detailed piers and half-timbered walls. Replacements for the modern-for-the-era metal casement windows and doors were difficult to locate but were eventually found in Birmingham, England.

This Norman-style home incorporates irregular massing and a gentle, low appearance; it requires the use of natural materials including slate roofs, brick, half-timbering, and stucco walls. These style characteristics were achieved in the major renovation of the garden façade by maintaining the unpretentious spirit of the floor jut-out with exposed joist ends supported on simulated stone piers. The new family room with covered porch extends the length of the rear façade and enhances the character of the original with the added accent of its tall-hipped slate roof.

On the front façade, the dramatic corner turret was converted into a children's playroom with interior walls detailed to resemble a fairy castle. The living room, dining room, and study required repair and careful restoration while other spaces required significant alterations or wholesale substitution. An entire suite of rooms replaced the original kitchen and laundry thereby opening up dated, small spaces to a flowing sequence of family room, kitchen/breakfast room, and sunroom—all opening to the newly created gardens and swimming pool.

Opposite
   Restored main façade
1   Site plan

1

2   Main level plan before renovation
3   Main level plan after renovation
4   Gallery and main stair
5   Dining room
6   Living room

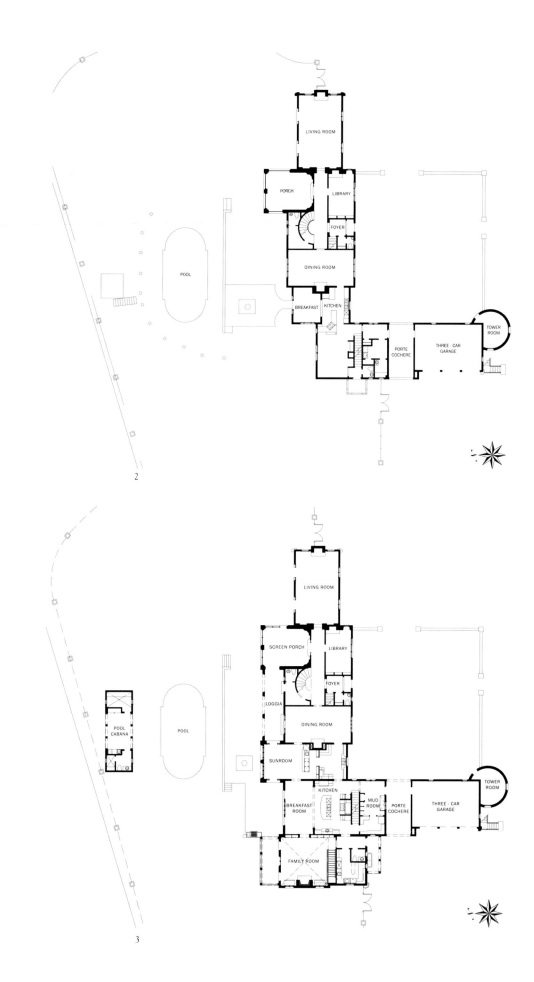

2

3

4

5

6

7

8

9

7   Family room
8   Family room with view of kitchen
9   New kitchen
10 New bar adjacent to kitchen
11 Restored porch with view of new loggia

10

11

12   Rear elevation before renovation
13   Rear elevation with new loggia and
     family room
14   Rear side before renovation
15   Previous bathroom add-on to house
16   Family room addition

12

13

14

15

16

West Paces Village
Erbesfield Residence, Atlanta, Georgia, 1999

Shaped by location and client preference, the appearance of this house is evocative of a modest country home in the Normandy region of France. The corner site influenced the L-shaped plan that provides privacy to the gardens, pool, and a separate garage connected by a covered breezeway. The use of irregular stone and brick walls, as well as the active massing of the slate roof, created a stylistic bond with the surrounding neighborhood. From the close view of the arrival court, the varied materials of herringbone-patterned brick mixed with Tennessee limestone and rough-quarried Alabama fieldstone help convey the fictional concept that the house is one of the estate buildings for the old French chateau located some distance away. The image of reuse of parts of the old chateau is furthered by the finely cut, but randomly assembled, limestone entry arch that in reality was carefully laid out on site by architect and mason. Small details like the plank door shutters and terra cotta chimney pots enhance the image of rural sophistication.

The interiors express the owners' passionate search for architectural antiques. The library, for example, was shaped to receive three walls collected from a chateau. The living room's design focuses on the intriguing hooded limestone fireplace that is enhanced by the raised paneled ceiling. The tall ceiling also provides space for twin antique carved-wood chandeliers. Other raised ceilings occur in the vaulted entry hall and the delicate handkerchief dome in the dining room.

The axis connecting the foyer through the living room expands outward in a jutting bay that provides a sunny informal sitting area and visual link to the gardens. From the living room and master bedroom, doors open onto the terraces. To the side, a second axis connects the breakfast room, pool, and Normandy-detailed pool house. The sloping site allowed for the location of the exercise room, wine cellar, and tasting room on the lower level.

Opposite
    Vaulted entry hall
1   Site plan

1

2   Main floor plan
3   Detail of main façade
Opposite
    Main façade from arrival court

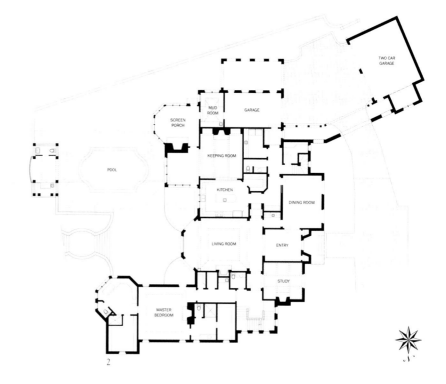

2

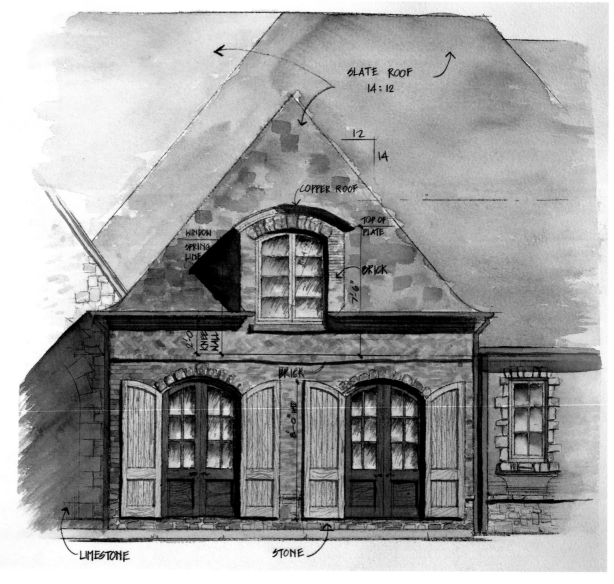

3

Opposite
    Living room coved ceiling and antique fireplace
6   Dining room
7   Living room

6

7

8

9

10

8   Keeping room
9   Breakfast room
10 Kitchen
11 Master bathroom
12 Master bedroom

11

12

14

Opposite
  Screen porch connecting keeping room and pool
14 Garden stair toward living room
15 Pool house
16 Rear elevation toward projecting living room

15

16

Erbesfield Residence   229

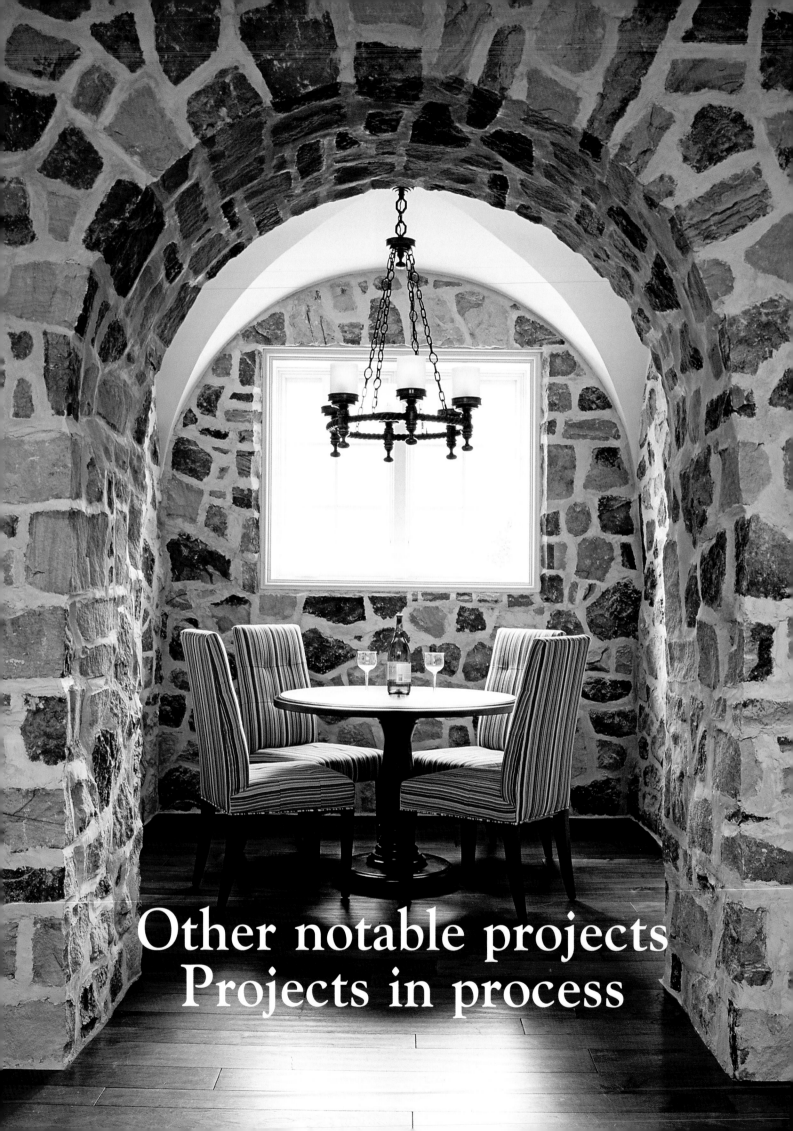

Other notable projects
Projects in process

Other notable projects

Habersham on Ivy, Atlanta, Georgia
19 four-story units, approximately 5,000 square feet each. Amenities include individual gardens, large terraces, elevators, gourmet kitchens, wine cellars, and media rooms.

American Carpenter Gothic Church Fellowship Hall, Monticello, Georgia
More than 5,000 square feet including kitchen, classrooms, and offices.

Island Design and Architectural Center (IDAC), St. Simons Island, Georgia
25,000 square feet of offices and home furnishings and decorative accessories showrooms.

Rumson Hall Town Homes, Atlanta, Georgia
17 four-story luxury town homes ranging in size from 4,300 to 5,500 square feet.

Inman Park Village, Atlanta, Georgia
19 town homes situated on a 20-acre redevelopment within the historic Inman Park neighborhood. Awards received include the 2007 Shutze Award for Multi-family Residential Design from the Institute of Classical Architecture & Classical America and the 2006 Design Excellence Award for New Construction by the Urban Design Commission.

Watersedge Town Homes, Jacksonville, Florida
20 Mediterranean-style town homes ranging from 2,500 to 3,000 square feet with amenities that include roof terraces with fireplaces, covered loggias, elevators, 12-foot main level ceilings, and detached garages that create private courtyards.

Game Day, Atlanta, Georgia
20,000-square-foot indoor sports training facility includes batting cages,
pitching tunnels, a short sprint track, weight room, artificial turf field,
arcade, party rooms, VIP room, as well as offices and a concessions area.

Georgian Residence, Atlanta, Georgia

Italianate Residence, Palmetto, Georgia

Greek Revival Residence, Sugar Hill, Georgia

Farmhouse, Ball Ground, Georgia

Regency Residence, Atlanta, Georgia

Alliance Children's Theatre Christmas House 2006,
Atlanta, Georgia

Portland Concrete 2001 Show House, Atlanta, Georgia

Norman-inspired Residence, Atlanta, Georgia

French Eclectic Residence, Atlanta, Georgia

Private Residence, Suwanee, Georgia

French Manor, Atlanta, Georgia

Private Residence, Atlanta, Georgia

2006 *Atlanta* Magazine Dream House, Atlanta, Georgia

Philadelphia-Style Arts & Crafts Residence, Atlanta, Georgia

1998 *Southern Accents*/Neiman Marcus Holiday House, Atlanta, Georgia

American Four-Square, Atlanta, Georgia

Georgian Residence, Atlanta, Georgia

EcoManor, Atlanta, Georgia
Recognized as the first home in Georgia to be LEED (Leadership in Energy and Environmental Design) certified by the U.S. Green Building Council.

French Eclectic Residence, Atlanta, Georgia

English Residence, Atlanta, Georgia

Mediterranean Beach Retreat, Sea Island, Georgia

English Country House, Atlanta, Georgia

Italianate Residence, Atlanta, Georgia

Neoclassical Residence, Atlanta, Georgia

Georgian Residence, McLean, Virginia

French Manor, Atlanta, Georgia

Private Residence, Atlanta, Georgia

French Eclectic Residence, Atlanta, Georgia

Arts & Crafts Residence, Atlanta, Georgia

English Country House, Alpharetta, Georgia

French Country House, Suwanee, Georgia

Beaux-Arts Residence, Birmingham, Alabama

French Country House, Atlanta, Georgia

Private Residence, Chattanooga, Tennessee

Private Residence, Atlanta, Georgia

Mediterranean Revival Residence, Atlanta, Georgia

Alliance Children's Theatre Christmas House 2005, Atlanta, Georgia

English Manor, Atlanta, Georgia

Mission Revival Gate House, Montecito, California

English Country House, Atlanta, Georgia

Tudor Residence, Atlanta, Georgia

Wilburn Revival Residence, Atlanta, Georgia

French Manor, Atlanta, Georgia

French Country House, Atlanta, Georgia

Arts & Crafts Residence, Atlanta, Georgia

Alliance Children's Theatre Christmas House 2004,
Atlanta, Georgia

Plantation Plain Revival Farmhouse, Madison, Georgia

Colonial Revival Farmhouse, Atlanta, Georgia

Greek Revival Residence, Atlanta, Georgia

Greek Revival Residence, Atlanta, Georgia

Colonial Revival Residence, Atlanta, Georgia

Modern River Dwelling, Blue Ridge, Georgia

Craftsman Bungalow, Atlanta, Georgia

Shingle-Style Cottage, Highlands, North Carolina

Mountain Rustic Retreat, Highlands, North Carolina

Stick-Style Boat House, Lake Burton, Georgia

Arts & Crafts Boat House, Madison, Georgia

Mountain Rustic Boat House, Lake Burton, Georgia

Rustic Eclectic Retreat, Lake Blue Ridge, Georgia

Woodhaven Bend Community Pavilion, Ball Ground, Georgia

Prairie-Style Residence, Atlanta, Georgia

Stone Cottage, Atlanta, Georgia

Florida Vernacular Beach Retreat, WaterColor, Florida

Community Pavilion and Boat House, Lake Rabun, Georgia

Florida Vernacular Beach Retreat, WaterColor, Florida

Florida Vernacular Beach Retreat, WaterColor, Florida

Florida Vernacular Beach Retreat, WaterColor, Florida

Florida Vernacular Beach Retreat, WaterColor, Florida

Florida Vernacular Beach Retreat, WaterColor, Florida

Private Residence, Atlanta, Georgia

English Country House, Atlanta, Georgia

Private Residence, Atlanta, Georgia

Shingle-Style Residence, Atlanta, Georgia

Craftsman-Style Retreat, Lake Burton, Georgia

2002 *Southern Accents* Highlands Cove Show House, Highlands, North Carolina

Shingle-Style Retreat, Greensboro, Georgia

Renovations

Before

Regency Residence, Columbus, Georgia

Before

Arts & Crafts Residence, Atlanta, Georgia

Before

Craftsman Cottage, Atlanta, Georgia

Before

English Manor, Atlanta, Georgia

Before   *House Beautiful* 2004 Makeover Showhouse, Chicago, Illinois

Before   **Rustic Retreat, Lake Burton, Georgia**

Before   **Private Residence, Atlanta, Georgia**

Before   **Craftsman Bungalow, Atlanta, Georgia**

Projects in process

English Cottages, Blue Ridge Golf & River Club, Blue Ridge, Georgia
20 rustic English cottages in four varied designs ranging from 1,200 to 1,500 square feet.

River Pavilion, Blue Ridge Golf & River Club, Blue Ridge, Georgia
5,000-square-foot, two-story community pavilion includes gathering space, boat storage, bar, outfitters shop, covered alfresco dining area with river views, catering kitchen, and locker rooms.

Gate House, Blue Ridge Golf & River Club, Blue Ridge, Georgia
Self-contained stone, timber, and shingle guard house.

Golf Learning Center, Blue Ridge Golf & River Club, Blue Ridge, Georgia
8,000-square-foot, two-story stone, timber, and shingle club house with member dining, pro shop, three golf training bays, management offices, and locker facilities.

Luxury Cottages, Greensboro, Georgia
40 rustic-style single-family homes in six varied designs ranging from 3,500 to 4,500 square feet. Exterior materials include shingle siding and stone cladding.

Luxury Duplexes, Greensboro, Georgia
50 rustic-style attached two-family homes in three alternate designs of approximately 3,300 square feet each.

Village Green Town Homes, Liberty Harbor, Brunswick, Georgia
16 four-story British Colonial-style town homes of approximately 3,000 square feet each with 10-foot ceilings, gourmet kitchens, breakfast rooms, private courtyards, loggias, and verandas.

Community Club House and Aquatic Center, Liberty Harbor, Brunswick, Georgia
20,000-square-foot community clubhouse with dining room, bar, banquet and meeting facilities, administrative offices, multiple swimming pools, locker rooms, loggias, verandas, and viewing tower.

River Crescent Neighborhood, Liberty Harbor, Brunswick, Georgia
Design of four plans for a neighborhood of detached single-family homes in the Liberty Harbor development. Plans range from 3,500 to 4,300 square feet and vary in style from Mediterranean to British Colonial with tastefully understated classical detailing.

Shingle-Style Residence, Liberty Harbor, Brunswick, Georgia

Bellingrath Town Residences, Atlanta, Georgia
Eight four-story town homes of approximately 7,000 square feet each that include roof terraces with fireplaces, covered loggias, elevators, and oversized master bedrooms with sitting areas.

Borghese Villas, Piazza at Paces, Atlanta, Georgia
24 four-story town homes ranging in size from 3,500 to 7,000 square feet.

City Place Town Homes, Atlanta, Georgia
Four-story modern town homes in multi-billion-dollar mixed-use project. 4,000-square-foot residences include roof terraces, interconnected multi-story volumes and large expanses of glass.

Winery, Lumpkin County, Georgia
25,000-square-foot Tuscan-style winery includes a tasting room, processing facility, gourmet restaurant, market, demonstration kitchen, and Owner's Club and private cellar.

The Mansion on Peachtree, Atlanta, Georgia
Design of floor plans and interiors for multiple luxury residences located within this 42-story building.

Angeles National Golf Club, Sunland, California
Associated with B3 Architects for a 27,000 square foot club house with pro shop, administrative offices, bar and dining room, kitchen, banquet room and cart storage.

Italianate Cottages, Lumpkin County, Georgia
Nine Tuscan-style weekend cottage designs range in size from 1,100 to 2,000 square feet.

Boys & Girls Club, Brunswick, Georgia
20,000-square-foot building includes a library, game room, music and digital photography lab, technology computer center, performance theater, and interior basketball court.

Italianate Villas, Lumpkin County, Georgia
13 different Italian villa designs, ranging in size from 2,600 to 5,800 square feet, contain gourmet kitchens, large entertaining spaces, and private courtyards.

Mediterranean-Style Mixed-Use Development, Montecito, California
18,000-square-foot project consists of retail space on the ground floor and ten luxury residences on the upper levels. Paseos, verandas, and loggias visually reduce the scale of the building, providing a relationship to the street and privacy for residents.

One Grant Park Condominiums, Atlanta, Georgia
Eight luxurious residences, each approximately 2,400 square feet, set above 2,000 square feet of commercial space and covered gated parking overlooking historic Grant Park.

Sonado Condominiums, Ft. Walton, Florida
20 four-story units, ranging in size from 600-square-foot studios to 2,600-square-foot, two-bedroom units.

Piedmont on Ansley, Atlanta, Georgia
18 mid-rise, luxury town homes ranging from 1,600-square-foot, two-bedroom units to 3,000-square-foot, three bedroom units.

Tate United Methodist Church, Tate, Georgia
Gothic Revival Church and 10,000-square-foot fellowship hall, classrooms, offices, kitchen, and meeting spaces.

Santa Barbara-Style Mixed-Use Development, Santa Barbara, California
Consisting of 1,000 square feet of office space and three residential units ranging from 1,200 to 2,500 square feet each, this project provides the transition to the area's commercial uses.

French Country Estate, McLean, Virginia

Santa Barbara Inn, Santa Barbara, California (Proposed)
55,000-square-foot, Mission Revival-Style Inn consists of 110 rooms, restaurant and bar, pool and spa, and banquet and conference facilities.

Tuscan-inspired Retreat, Frederica Township, St. Simons Island, Georgia

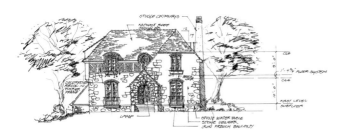

Avignon Community Club House, Vinings, Georgia
3,500-square-foot club house with sitting area, wine room, catering kitchen, exercise room with spa, steam room, and outdoor pool.

Georgian Residence, Atlanta, Georgia

English Manor, Roswell, Georgia

Regency Residence, Atlanta, Georgia

English Manor, Alpharetta, Georgia

Mountain Rustic Retreat, Bend, Oregon

Arts & Crafts Lake Retreat, Lake Norman, North Carolina

French Country Home, Marietta, Ohio

Palladian Villa, Sea Island, Georgia

French Colonial Home on Tuggle Creek, Reynolds Plantation, Greensboro, Georgia

English Manor, Bend, Oregon

French Country Home, Atlanta, Georgia

English Manor, Atlanta, Georgia

Spanish Villa, McLean, Virginia

Colonial Revival Residence, Greenwich, Connecticut

English Manor, Atlanta, Georgia

Modern Residence, Santa Barbara, California

French Eclectic Residence, Suwanee, Georgia

Arts & Crafts Residence, Newton County, Georgia

Beach Retreat at Frederica Township, St. Simons Island, Georgia

French Country Home, McLean, Virginia

French Manor, Suwanee, Georgia

Italian Renaissance Villa, Chattanooga, Tennessee

Arts & Crafts Residence, Alpharetta, Georgia

Italian Villa, Palm Beach, Florida

French Country Home, Greenville, North Carolina

Avignon Town Homes, Vinings, Georgia
85 new town homes recreate the image of a French hill town. Ranging
from 3,000 to 4,000 square feet, these town homes are situated in 21
buildings of rustic limestone, tumbled weathered brick, and distressed wood
timbers with copper metal details.

Mediterranean Villa, Bel Air, California

Acknowledgments

Harrison Design Associates
Management

Principals

William H. Harrison

Gregory L. Palmer

Anthony P. Spann

Business Principal

Deborah Hodge Harrison

Finance and Marketing Associates

S. Josie Capps

Joni C. Emerson

Carol A. Hayes

Melissa M. Wilson

Design Associates

John J. Albanese

Edward J. Alshut

Bernard J. Austin

Bulent A. Baydar

Dawn M. Bennett

Geoffry P. Borwick

Glen G. Deisler

Karen H. Ferguson

David T. Falk

Chad E. Goehring

Adele S. Goggia

Richard C. Hatch

R. Derek Hopkins

Deitrich T. Logan

Barbara C. Lowenthal

Steven L. Markey

Robert C. Pich

Susanne Kortz Tejada

Robert A. Tretsch III

Harrison Design Associates
East Coast

Fourth (back) row, left to right
Robert S. Cooney, Nathaniel A. Lawson, Kent M. Nelson, William T. Exum, Robert A. Tretsch III, Gregory L. Palmer, John J. Albanese, Robert C. Pich, Robert H. Smith, Miroslawa L. Irlik, J. Martin Rodriguez, Richard C. Hatch, Chad E. Goehring

Third row, left to right
Robert Entenza, Joshua S. Hunt, Franklin M. Heery, Jose J. Reyes, Visut Kromadit, R. Derek Hopkins, Geoffrey P. Borwick, Dietrich T. Logan, J. Ryan Hopwood, Darius D. Stewart, Jonathan N. Park, Stefanie A. Wahl, Bryan C. Looney, Joni C. Emerson, Edward J. Alshut

Second row, left to right
Benjamin L. Robbins, Caroline B. Tezza, Yuko Hattori, Karen H. Ferguson, Suzanne M. Hearn, Bulent A. Baydar, Julia A. Praser, Kazunari Aiba, Lee F. Brooks, William H. Harrison, Katharine M. Andersen, S. Josie Capps, Teresa N. Snider, Angela J. Janesheski, Dawn M. Bennett, Kittipat Robkob, Carmin R. Ogata

Front row, left to right
Sonia Markey, Steven L. Markey, Amanda W. Kanabe, Virginia K. Ramirez, Catherine L. Schreiman, Lidia Bakun, Ann E. Sample, Heather R. Brown, Lindsay A. Weiss, Deborah Hodge Harrison, Carol A. Hayes, Allyson W. Barfoot, Saipin Chulacharitta, Gregory C. Mix, Miriam D. Mantius, Nicole C. Haskins, Jennifer L. Harris, Melissa M. Wilson

Harrison Design Associates
West Coast

Back row, left to right
Marc J. Compton, Glen G. Deisler, Juan Carlos
Buitrago, Anthony P. Spann, Adele S. Goggia,
Mark V. Quinn

Middle row, left to right
Susanne Kortz Tejada, Jose L. Gomez, Barbara
C. Lowenthal, Bernard J. Austin

Front row, left to right
Angelina A. Reyes, Anthony F. Grumbine, Nick
Chatwatanasiri, David T. Falk

Allied Professionals

"Without craftsmanship, inspiration is a mere reed shaken in the wind." Johannes Brahms

Clients' visions and a passion for classical design are the driving inspirations behind each Harrison Design Associates' project. To produce commissions of the quality and complexity featured in this monograph requires not only a strong building design, but more importantly, a team of talented professionals from many fields, working together to achieve a common goal. It is with sincerest thanks that we recognize the following contractors, interior designers, landscape architects and designers, specialty consultants and illustrators, without whom our work would simply not be possible.

Abate Landscape & Garden Design, Charlotte, North Carolina
Debbie Anderson, Atlanta, Georgia
Arcadia Studio, Santa Barbara, California
Artisan Builders, LLC, McLean, Virginia
Ashe Construction, Inc., Cashiers, North Carolina
Associated Custom Builders, LLC, McLean, Virginia
Atlanta Fine Gardens, Atlanta, Georgia
B+C Studio, Atlanta, Georgia
B3 Architects, Santa Barbara, California
Barry Dixon Inc., Warrenton, Virginia
Beecham Builders, LLC, Alpharetta, Georgia
Benecki Fine Homes, Atlanta, Georgia
Bentley Properties, (Ted Jacobson), Atlanta, Georgia
Bildon Construction & Development, (Rick Fierer), Atlanta, Georgia
Black Rock Construction, Bend, Oregon
Bradford R. Davis, Inc., Destin Florida
Breaux Construction, Santa Rosa Beach, Florida
Brompton Property, Chicago, Illinois
Brookwood Kitchens Inc., Atlanta, Georgia
Jaques Brunet, Atlanta, Georgia
Brunning & Stang, Atlanta, Georgia
Budd & Stormont Builders, Atlanta, Georgia
By Hammer & Hand Builders, Atlanta, Georgia
C.H. Eaton Enterprises Inc., (Howard Eaton), Lavonia, Georgia
Capitella Homes Ltd., Suwannee, Georgia
Dan Carithers, Atlanta, Georgia
Carole Weaks Interiors, Atlanta, Georgia
Cascade Design Group, Atlanta, Georgia
Cascade Design Group, Bellingham, Washington
Casey Studio, (Rick Casey), Smyrna, Georgia
Cheryl Lucas Interior Design, San Francisco, California
Christy Dillard Design, Atlanta, Georgia
Clark and White Landscape, Los Angeles, California
Clay Construction, Rabun County, Georgia
CMI Interiors, Inc., Atlanta, Georgia
Colonnade Custom Homes, Inc., Atlanta, Georgia
Columbus Cook, Atlanta, Georgia
Cook Bonner Construction, Atlanta, Georgia
Craftmaster, (Ed Levin), Atlanta, Georgia
Crane Joint Venture, California
Culliton Quinn Landscape Architecture Workshop, Chicago, Illinois
Dargan Landscape Architects, Atlanta, Georgia
Daria Designs, Atlanta, Georgia
David H. Mitchell & Associates, Washington, D.C.
David Henson Interiors, Atlanta, Georgia

Delany Rossetti Construction, Atlanta, Georgia
Dernehl Inc., Marietta, Georgia
The Design Atelier Inc., (Melanie Millner), Atlanta, Georgia
Design Galleria, Atlanta, Georgia
Design Innovations, Atlanta, Georgia
DES-SYN, Atlanta, Georgia
Dilger-Gibson Inc., Atlanta, Georgia
Douglas Herrin, Inc., Atlanta, Georgia
Durek Construction, Brunswick, Georgia
E. Graham Pittman & Associates, Inc., Smyrna, Georgia
Ed Castro Landscape, Inc., Roswell, Georgia
Chris Edwards, Santa Barbara, California
EPID Co. Inc., Atlanta, Georgia
Ann Erbesfield, Atlanta, Georgia
Essary & Murphy, Inc. Atlanta, Georgia
Euro Homes Inc., Alpharetta, Georgia
Fine Landscapes, Ltd., Great Falls, Virginia
Ed and Fred Foster, Birmingham, Alabama
Franklin-Caldwell, Atlanta, Georgia
Gair Landscaping Co., Inc., Smyrna, Georgia
Gallo Contracting, (Joe Romano), Atlanta, Georgia
Gibbs Landscape Co., Smyrna, Georgia
Giffin & Crane, Santa Barbara, California
Holly Greene, Marietta, Georgia
Greenfield Construction, Duluth, Georgia
Guyton Design Group, Atlanta, Georgia
Harbor View Group Holdings, LLC, St. Simons Island, Georgia
Harrison Design Associates Interiors, Atlanta, Georgia
Andrea Henslick, Atlanta, Georgia
HGOR, Atlanta, Georgia
Highgrove Partners, Alpharetta, Georgia
Holcombe Associates, Birmingham, Alabama
Alan D. Holt, ASLA, Landscape Architect, Panama City, Florida
Huff-Dewberry, LLC, Atlanta, Georgia
Image Homes, Atlanta, Georgia
Interior Views, Atlanta, Georgia
In-Town Development Group, LLC, Atlanta, Georgia
J.D. Group Inc., Los Angeles, California
J.F. Hearn, Inc., Atlanta, Georgia
J.W.B. Properties, (Jim Brown), Atlanta, Georgia
Jackie Cotrill LLC, Atlanta, Georgia
Jacquelynne P. Lanham Designs, Atlanta, Georgia
James Dean Design, Thousand Oaks, California
James Michael Howard Inc., Jacksonville, Florida
Jane J. Marsden Interiors and Antiques, Atlanta, Georgia
Daryl Jennings, Chattanooga, Tennessee

Jerrel Griffin Construction, Inc. California
Jie Jiao, Atlanta, Georgia
Joe A. Gayle & Associates, Atlanta, Georgia
John Oetgen Interiors, Atlanta, Georgia
Johnson, William & Harris LLC, Atlanta, Georgia
Jones & Jones, Madison, Georgia
Julian LeCraw Construction, Atlanta, Georgia
Kairos Development, Atlanta, Georgia
Keller Outdoor Inc., Chatsworth, Georgia
Elizabeth Koets, Atlanta, Georgia
Lakeland Luxury Inc., Charlotte, North Carolina
Land Plus Associates Ltd., Atlanta, Georgia
Landtrack Properties, Inc., Atlanta, Georgia
Susan Lapelle, Atlanta, Georgia
LeBlanc/Crooks, Atlanta, Georgia
Leigh Nunnery Interiors, Atlanta, Georgia
Lisa Torbett Interiors, St. Simons Island, Georgia
Live Oaks Development, St. Simons, Georgia
Liz Williams Interiors, Atlanta, Georgia
M. Deane Johnson, Inc., Atlanta, Georgia
Marcia Singleton Designs, Alpharetta, Georgia
Mario Nievera Design Inc., Palm Beach, Florida
Dan Mattox & James Cotton, Builders II, Atlanta, Georgia
mB3: Julie Devita Interior Design, St. Simons Island, Georgia
Meridy W. King Interiors, Atlanta, Georgia
Meritt Construction, Suwannee, Georgia
Michael Jackson Landscape Co. Inc., Atlanta, Georgia
Michael King Construction, LLC, Calhoun, Georgia
The Miller Design Group, Chatsworth, Georgia
Monkey Business Interiors, Inc., Marietta, Georgia
Monte Hewett Homes, Santa Rosa, Florida
Multiscape, Inc., Norcross, Georgia
N. Roberts Inc., Atlanta, Georgia
Nancy Braithwaite Interiors, Atlanta, Georgia
Nevin Interior Design, Atlanta, Georgia
Noles Services Lawn & Landscape, Iron Station, North Carolina
Katie O'Reilly Rogers, ASLA, Santa Barbara, California
Owings & Aeschlimann, LLC, Suwannee, Georgia
Pace-Knight Inc., Atlanta, Georgia
Mark A. Palmer, Atlanta, Georgia
Patricia McLean Interiors, Atlanta, Georgia
Peace Design, Atlanta, Georgia
The Peachtree Group, Atlanta, Georgia
Pease Construction Inc., St. Simons Island, Georgia
Phoenix Ironworks, (Corrina Mensoff), Atlanta, Georgia
Planters, Inc., Atlanta, Georgia
Potts General Contractors, Conyers, Georgia
R.E. Truskowski Landscape Architects, Laguna Beach, California
R.M. Bondurant Construction Inc., Atlanta, Georgia
Ramey Construction, Clayton, Georgia

Reese, Hoopes and Fincher, Inc., Atlanta, Georgia
The Renaissance Corporation, (Warren Sirzyk), Atlanta, Georgia
Richard Anderson Landscape Architects, Atlanta, Georgia
Richard W. Greene Inc., Marietta, Georgia
The Rime Companies, Birmingham, Alabama
Rob Marrett Custom Homes, Sea Island, Georgia
Robert Brown Interior Design, Duluth, Georgia
Roberta Sirzyk Interiors, Atlanta, Georgia
Robin Burnette Interiors, Atlanta, Georgia
Rose Kastle Inc., (Doug Rose), Atlanta, Georgia
Russell P. Bencaz & Associates, Naples, Florida
Scapes, LLC, Marietta, Georgia
Scott Contracting, Duluth, Georgia
Sea Island Landscape, Sea Island, Georgia
Toni Facella Sensi, Rome, Italy
SFA Design, Santa Barbara, California
Shane Meder & Associates, Atlanta, Georgia
Site Solutions LLC, Atlanta, Georgia
Southeastern Construction & Management, Atlanta, Georgia
Stan Topol & Associates, Atlanta, Georgia
Stanley Ellis Inc., Mobile, Alabama
Lou Stormont, Atlanta, Georgia
Michael Stouse, New Orleans, Louisiana
Studio D+C, Atlanta, Georgia
Susan B. Bozeman Designs, Inc., Atlanta, Georgia
Susan S. Young Designs, Chattanooga, Tennessee
Suzanne Kasler Interiors, Atlanta, Georgia
Tapie Construction, (Matt Tapie), Newbury Park, California
Thomas Landscaping, Atlanta, Georgia
Tim Wolf Design and Landscape, Atlanta, Georgia
Tom Lennon Company, Atlanta, Georgia
Tom Williams Residential, Sandy Springs, Georgia
George Tomola, Atlanta, Georgia
Tunnell & Tunnell Landscape Architecture, Atlanta, Georgia
Tyler Development Corporation, California
Unique Housing Concepts, Suwannee, Georgia
Valerie Parkinson Interiors, Atlanta, Georgia
Vantosh & Associates, Atlanta, Georgia
Vaughan Home Builders, Atlanta, Georgia
Viridis Garden Designs Inc., Atlanta, Georgia
Susan Wagoner, Naples, Florida
Walter McDonald & Co., Atlanta, Georgia
Nancy Warren, Atlanta, Georgia
Ann Warsham, Atlanta, Georgia
Will Goodman & Associates, Atlanta, Georgia
William Huff Interiors, Columbus, Georgia
Wood+Partners Inc., Hilton Head, South Carolina
Woodall Construction, Tiger, Georgia
Wright Brothers Builders Inc., Westport, Connecticut

Photography credits

Unless otherwise indicated, all site and floor plans, detail renderings, drawings, and watercolor renderings by Harrison Design Associates.

Front and back jacket: John Umberger
Page 1: Jim Bartsch
Page 2–3, 8: John Umberger
Page 6: Emily Minton-Redfield for *Traditional Home*

Paces End Manor
All photography by John Umberger

Cima Vista
Jim Bartsch: 24–25, 26, 29 (7), 30, 32 (15), 34
Gordon Beall for *Traditional Home*: 28, 29 (6), 31, 32 (13,14), 33, 35

Hawn Residence
John Umberger: 36–37, 40 (4), 41, 42 (7,9), 43, 44 (13), 45, 48 (23), 49
Harrison Design Associates: 38, 40 (2,5), 44 (12)
Gil Stose: 42 (8), 44 (11), 46, 47 (20)
Lynn McGill: 47 (18,19)
Michael Parker: 48 (22)

Paces End Estate
John Umberger: 50–51, 52, 54, 55, 59
Jonathan Harper: 57
Harrison Design Associates: 58

Georgian Residence
All photography by John Umberger

Riddle Beach Retreat
All photography by William Waldron for *Southern Accents*

English Manor
John Umberger: 80–81, 82, 84, 85, 86, 87, 89 (14)
Harrison Design Associates: 88, 89 (12,13)

Hacienda Hermosa
Franco Rossi: 90–91, 92, 94, 95, 96 (7), 97, 99 (11), 101
Eric Scott: 96 (6), 98–99 (10,12), 100

Cohen Lake Retreat
Gil Stose: 102–103, 106, 107, 108, 109, 110, 111 (12,13)
John Umberger: 104
Lynn McGill: 111 (11)

All'Ombra
Emily Minton-Redfield for *Traditional Home*: 112–113, 117, 118, 119 (8), 120 (10)
Boutchine Studios: 114, 121 (13), 122 (14,16,17)
Lynn McGill: 119 (6,7)
John Umberger: 120 (9), 121 (11,12), 123
Harrison Design Associates: 122 (15)

Spring Hill Farm
Tria Giovan for *Southern Accents*: 124–125, 128, 129, 130, 131, 132, 133 (10,11,12), 134, 135
Boutchine Studios: 126, 133 (13)

Echols Residence
John Umberger: 136–137, 138, 140 (3), 141, 142, 143, 144 (10)
Harrison Design Associates: 140 (4), 144 (9)

Miller Residence
Fred Gerlich: 146–147, 148, 150, 151, 152, 153, 155 (12)
John Umberger for Trends Publishing International: 154, 155 (10,11)

Acheson Residence
All photography by John Umberger except 165 (8) by Harrison Design Associates

Sturm Residence
Fred Gerlich: 172–173, 176, 178 (5), 179 (7), 180, 181 (11)
Boutchine Studios: 174, 178 (4), 179 (8), 181 (12)
John Umberger: 177, 179 (6)

Cannon Residence
All photography by John Umberger

Azalea House Renovation
All photography by Boutchine Studios

West Paces Village Overview
John Umberger: 202–203, 211
Harrison Design Associates: 204, 205, 207
Scott Francis: 206
Boutchine Studios: 208, 209, 210

West Paces Village – Richardson Franklin House Renovation
All photography by John Umberger

West Paces Village – Erbesfield Residence
All photography by John Umberger, except 229 (16) by John Umberger for Trends Publishing International

The following former Harrison Design Associates employees also contributed to the body of work within this book:
Timothy S. Adams, Suvi M. Bayly, Cameron Bird, Blair Blair, David Bolus, Neil O. Campbell, Scott C. Carlyle, Chiu Ching-Chi, Joseph Claghorn, Quintus C. Colbert, Prajakta S. Dabhade, Robin M. Fierer, Paul Geary, Walt Greene, Glen G. Grimwood, Lucas P. Hafeli, Heather D. Harrison, Craig A. Headrick, Scott J. Hill, Nuchanat Intaragumhaeng, Kyle V. Kessler, Kil Ko Kim, Perry W. Kelly, C. Michael Kleeman, Glenn A. Larrimore, Boyd H. Leyburn, Elizabeth A. Looney, Leah J. Mannheimer, Kerry L. Martin, Fern Merinoff, Amy D. Palmer, Zoran S. Pericic, David Pursley, Steven S. Register, Christopher Rhinehart, Gillian Rodrigues, Kittiphun Sereeviriyakul, Sara J. Shirley, Steven Shockley, Adam Stillman, Nathan P. Streets, Richard J. Tancini, Chatima Wannapaiboon, Jay A. Waronker, Nicklaus J. Wilt, Reid D. Wood